LIFE UNDER THE TUDORS

KT-398-509

THE FALCON HISTORIES
Edited by J. E. Morpurgo

LIFE UNDER THE STUARTS

Forthcoming
LIFE IN EIGHTEENTH-CENTURY BRITAIN

25481

LIFE UNDER THE TUDORS

WORKING MEN'S COLLEGE LIBRARY

LONDON

FALCON EDUCATIONAL BOOKS

First published in 1950
by Falcon Educational Books
6 & 7 Crown Passage, Pall Mall,
London, S.W.1

Printed in Great Britain
by the Peregrine Press Limited
Widnes

All rights reserved

Copyright 1950
by Falcon Educational Books

AUSTRALIA
The Invincible Press
Sydney, Melbourne, Brisbane, Adelaide

NEW ZEALAND
The Invincible Press, Wellington

CANADA
The Falcon Press
263-7 Adelaide Street West, Toronto

SOUTH AFRICA
M. Darling (Pty.) Ltd., Cape Town

CONTENTS

CONTENTS

ILLUSTRATIONS

ILLUSTRATIONS

I

ENGLAND UNDER THE TUDORS

CHRISTOPHER MORRIS

No historian of Tudor England can hope to change what is, quite literally, our view of sixteenth-century people: that has been fixed for all time by Holbein and his poorer imitators. We can only see what the portrait-painters were paid to see on our behalf; and most of the sitters now appear to us as dolls overdressed in flamboyant clothes. They look sour and wooden, hard-featured or indeed black-avised. They are thin-lipped and pig-eyed. They are cruel, covetous, brazen, florid and terrifyingly intelligent; but never candid, never kindly. The women seem minxes, the poets fops, the soldiers bravos; the reformers seem merely stubborn, the states-men merely sly. The scholars are made pedants and the saints fanatics. Who could guess from their pictures at Tyndale's genius or at More's vivacity? It is well that there is no indubitable Shakespeare portrait to fall like a curtain between us and his works. It is fortunate, too, that we have ears to hear, for Tudor music reaches us with less distortion. And the music is softer and gentler than the paintings. There is humanity and even heart-

9

ache in the madrigals and canzonets; and Tudor harshness suffers a sea-change in the haunting melodies of *The Silver Swan* or *My Lady Greensleeves*.

On the surface too the Tudor story is a stark and fierce one, turning as it does so largely on the Great Pillage, on the Fires of Smithfield and on the fate of Mary Stuart. Some of the protagonists—Wolsey and Cromwell, Northumberland and Leicester—were little more than shameless adventurers. The two great kings can appear monsters of avarice or of lust. Burghley the greatest statesman of the century and Bacon its greatest thinker were shifty, calculating wordlings. Drake was a pirate and Hawkins began the slave trade. Essex, the popular romantic hero, had a vulgar film-star temperament which brought him to the block. Marlowe was a spy and perished in a tavern brawl. Surrey, another poet of great promise, was beheaded. Peter Wentworth, champion of parliamentary freedom, rotted to death in the Tower. More died on the scaffold, Latimer at the stake; so did Tyndale the father of the English Bible, and Cranmer chief author of the English Prayer Book. The saintly Campion and the sweet poet Southwell were racked and disembowelled. No wonder that Nashe's *Unfortunate Traveller,* the first best-selling English novel, was a procession of protracted deaths. No wonder the playgoers called for plots thickened with treachery, cruelty and revenge. The same violence prevailed in religious or even in literary controversy. We cannot read without embarrassment the Billingsgate which More levelled against Tyndale, and we should remember that 'gentle Shakespeare' was once bound over to keep the peace.

Against this background it is almost startling to read in the Prologue to Colet's grammar for his new school,

St. Paul's, 'I pray you, all little babies, all little children, learn gladly this little treatise . . . Trusting of this beginning that ye shall proceed and grow to perfect literature, and come at the last to be great clerks. And lift up your little white hands for me, which prayeth for you to God'; or to find Hooker shrinking from sectarian conflict and asking to 'be removed into some quiet country parsonage, where I may see God's blessings spring out of my mother earth, and eat mine own bread in peace and privacy'. Without Shakespeare's help we should often be unmindful of the quiet humdrum simplicities behind the turmoil and truculence of much Tudor life. But we have the Forest of Arden—a real place in Shakespeare's county —as well as the courts of Elsinore and Dunsinane. London was before long to be the biggest city in Europe, but the vast majority of Englishmen were still country-bred; and it was necessary, when Leicester took them to the wars in Flanders, to ordain that 'in marching by the fields, no man at the putting up of any hare or other beast shall make any shout or cry, whereby to disquiet the rest of the bands'.

Yet Shakespeare can give us a false sense of knowing Tudor men and women when in reality we do not. The difficulties in our way are serious, for the age had very real paradoxes, complexities and contradictions. Its shadows can only be illumined by fitful and by artificial lights. We are easily tempted to be wise after the event, to suppose that what followed the Tudors was intended by them. Or we may fall into judging life from literature, forgetting that to write at all is to be a little unorthodox and that a writer is often moved by a restless spirit that looks forward or backward into some anachronistic world. It was peculiarly true of Tudor England that in the same society, or even in the same man, the conservative and the radical rubbed shoulders; so did credulity and scepticism, confidence and diffidence, bellicosity and love of peace, the pride of being 'mere English' and the crying up of foreign wares. Nor must we overlook the curious time-lag which governed the period. Half of the sixteenth century was spent before Tudor England had noticeably acquired the main characteristics that we now call 'Tudor'; and half of Elizabeth's reign before the poets and adventurers made it 'Elizabethan'.

It is even more important to remember how much of mediæval civilization survived throughout the century. At the dissolution of the monasteries the nuns of Lacock Abbey still spoke Norman-French. Although football in a recognizably modern form had appeared before Elizabeth's accession—and the first reliable reference to cricket—tournaments between knights in armour were still going on when the Queen died. Ascham and others still looked on the long bow as the Englishman's stock weapon and it was issued to militiamen until the time of the Armada. As late as 1621 an archbishop missed a deer and killed a gamekeeper with a cross-bow bolt. Much of Tudor architecture was a variation on the Gothic perpendicular theme. King's College Chapel was finished under Henry VIII, as was Bath Abbey and the tower at Fountains; and the basic form of many a Tudor hall or mansion is that of a somewhat ill-defended castle. Very little 'Renaissance' design appeared in printing or in wood or stone or plaster before 1530 and nearly all of it can be traced to foreign workmen. The best native painters were miniaturists whose work is in line with Gothic illumination. In spite of far-reaching economic change, all parties paid lip-service at the very least to the traditional view that taking interest was the sin of usury. Everyone still believed, consciously or unconsciously, in the mediæval universe with its four elements, its wet and dry humours, its planetary spheres and influences. The framework within which Hooker built his philosophy was a framework taken over from Aquinas. Spenser, it is true, was aware that he was writing the *Faerie Queene* for a new kind of man, in fact for the first generation of English gentlemen, but he looked to them to revive the chivalry of a more golden world. Much of his outlook was bound up in his belief that 'world' derived from 'warre-old', something which got worse as it got older.

At Cambridge in Spenser's time most young men were less conservative. The demand was all for 'new books, new fashions, new laws, new officers, and some after new elements, some after new heavens and hells too. Turkish affairs familiarly known: castles built in the air'. So wrote Spenser's friend, cantankerous Gabriel Harvey. Yet the castles and the new worlds were a long time building. It is significant that in the Tudor litany which we still use, we pray for the magistrates to be given grace 'to maintain truth'—not to encourage the search after new truths but to maintain the truth already known. The religious Reformers claimed always to be restoring the lost truths once known to the primitive Church. Much the same view was taken of the laws. Parliament was not conscious of creating new law; it was a High Court declaring what the law—divine, natural, fundamental, customary—already was and always had been. Even the so-called New Monarchy was not very new and invented no new machinery of government. It merely made the old machinery work. The coming revolutions which made England a 'free country' did so by retaining for the nation her mediæval

13

freedoms at a time when other nations were becoming up-to-date by losing theirs. England has a constitutional monarchy, parliamentary government and 'the rule of law' by virtue of being the one country that remained mediæval.

The Middle Ages might almost be defined as the ages in which an illiterate laity had to be civilized and educated through the eye, by ritual and emblems, by pageantry and heraldry. Every story had to be pictorial. Although literacy increased fast under the Tudors, men did not cease to use their eyes in the old way. Hence the pomps and progresses kept up by Tudor courts, the Field of the Cloth of Gold and Queen Elizabeth's two thousand dresses. It proved possible to give the Anglican Church a Protestant theology because theology is something men cannot see. But they can see what goes on in the chancel of their parish church, and in such things are apt to be conservative. Hence the retention of so much of the Catholic liturgy by the new Church of England. Throughout the period plays were still things to be seen and not read. Many have been lost because never printed, and twenty-one of Shakespeare's plays had not been printed when he died. It is said that on the eve of Essex's abortive rising, the rebels bribed the players to act *Richard II*. We are puzzled, because to read the play is to see that the king has the best poetry and that the general tone seems sentimentally royalist. But the spectacle is different. What the audience sees is a weak king failing to rise to the occasion and being publicly dethroned.

Of course literacy and learning were growing and held much in honour. Education lost something when the monasteries were dissolved but gained more from the foundation of the new grammar schools. These provided something of a career open to the talents. 'He kept me to school,' said Latimer of his yeoman father, 'or else I had not been able to have preached before the king's majesty now'. Tudor education was surprisingly democratic, for the clever children of all classes could go to school together. So great was the respect for learning that Nicholas Udall, author of *Ralph Roister Doister* the first extant English comedy, was made Headmaster of Westminster under Mary Tudor in spite of having written Protestant pamphlets and in spite of having ceased to be Headmaster of Eton because he stole the college plate. Lady Jane Grey did not seem priggish to her tutor Roger Ascham when she said, 'I wis, all their sport in the Park is but a shadow to that pleasure that I find in Plato'. We must remember that the rediscovery of Plato was still a new adventure, although education was pursued mainly for its supposed practical utility. For long it was held that if princes and gentlemen were given the right education all else in the commonwealth would go well; and in England a small literature grew up in imitation of Castiglione's *Courtier*. This belief was shaken by the coming of Protestant pessimism with its emphasis upon original sin. If fallen man was totally depraved he might also be presumed ineducable. Yet in time the Protestants, by making men feel that they had to save their own souls instead of looking to Mother Church to do it for them, made them also think of fitting themselves by education for this grave responsibility.

Not all the educationalists were solely concerned with the classics or the Scriptures. Some were stirred by a new awareness of the English tongue. The language was quite visibly adding cubits to its stature all through Tudor times. Even minor writers like Harvey, Nashe or Puttenham invented dozens of the words we use. 'I honour the Latin, but I worship the English.' So wrote Spenser's headmaster at Merchant Taylors', Richard Mulcaster. And he goes on, 'But why not all in English, a tongue of itself both deep in conceit, and frank in delivery? I do not think that any language, be it whatsoever, is better able to utter all arguments, either with more pith, or greater plainness, than our English tongue is'.

Learning was credited with miraculous powers. 'For,' wrote Bacon, 'nothing parcel of the world is denied to man's inquiry and invention. . . . There is no danger at all in the proportion or quantity of knowledge, how large soever. . . . By learning man ascendeth to the heavens and their motions, where in body he cannot come.' One man of really great capacity, a Hooker or a Robert Burton, could still master and integrate almost all the knowledge in Europe. The floods of new knowledge had not yet burst their banks and, for a few years, men did not feel adrift or overwhelmed. It was not until 1623 that William Drummond was to write that 'Sciences, by the diverse motions of this globe of the brain of man, are become opinions, nay, errors, and leave the imagination in a thousand labyrinths. What is all we know, compared with what we know not?' Knowledge, to the Elizabethans, seemed manageable and did not yet seem 'academic'. On the contrary it was thought to bear directly upon 'reality' and even upon action. By knowledge, thought Bacon, 'contemplation and action may be more nearly and straitly conjoined and united together than they have been. . . . Knowledge may not be, as a courtesan, for pleasure and vanity only . . . but as a spouse, for generation, fruit and comfort'. Nor did learning, in Tudor England, always mean book-learning. Ascham might regret that 'the young gentlemen of England go so unwillingly to school, and run so fast to the stable', but he said expressly, 'I do not mean that young gentlemen should always be poring on a book'. They 'should use and delight in all courtly exercises and gentlemanlike pastime. . . . For the Muses, besides learning, were also ladies of dancing, mirth and minstrelsy: Apollo was god of shooting and author of cunning playing upon instruments: Pallas also was lady mistress in wars'. We are apt to forget that Hamlet was an athlete. 'It is not a mind,' said Mulcaster, 'not a body, that we have to educate, but a man; and we cannot divide him'.

Belief in education means believing in the future. 'You suppose', wrote Harvey to Spenser, 'the first age was the gold age. It is nothing so. Bodin defendeth the gold age to flourish now, and our own first grandfathers to have rubbed through in the iron and brazen age at the beginning when all things were rude and unperfect in comparison of the exquisite fineness and delicacy we are grown unto at these days.' Most Tudor intellectuals despised or patronized the past. Ascham said that 'the whole pleasure' to be found in the *Morte d'Arthur* 'standeth in open mans slaughter and bold bawdry'. Sidney apologized for his 'barbarousness' when he confessed 'I never heard the old song of Percy and Douglas, that I found not my heart moved more than with a trumpet', although the song was 'so evil apparelled in the dust and cobwebs of that uncivil age'.

There was some justification for the Elizabethans' belief in their own age. The ruthless work of Henry VII and of Henry VIII had remodelled English society and given it enough stability and order for men to feel rooted and secure. Yet neither the new ruling classes nor the new monarchy felt very firmly in the saddle. Neither could afford to be tyrannical. The Protestants dared not perse-

B

cute the Old Religion too severely. The gentry had to make a Poor Law that was not over-harsh in its treatment of the unemployed. The aristocracy could not close its ranks to keep out successful merchants or servants of the Crown. Antonio with his fortunes floating in his 'argosies' and Othello who had 'done the State some service' move as equals among Venetian gentlemen. Much was said about observing 'degree, priority and place', but in practice Tudor society remained fluid. Its cult of the goddess Fortune shows awareness of how dramatically men could rise and fall. A yeoman's son like Drake could become an Admiral; and a successful playwright could become the owner of New Place at Stratford, and of a coat of arms. Ben Jonson dined once with the Earl of Salisbury, but found himself seated well below the salt and served from separate dishes; yet he felt free to call out 'My Lord, you promised that I should dine with you, but I do not'.

Something of the same fluidity, the same unwillingness to define or to draw hard-and-fast lines, prevailed in Tudor politics. The Tudors behaved despotically but were despots mainly by sheer force of personality. They had not the machinery of despotism, the standing army, the police force, the large-scale bureaucracy. These were luxuries they were too poor to afford.* Inevitably the 'despotism' was amateurish, not professional, dependent in large measure on the goodwill of the Justice of the Peace. Besides, no ruler could bring about any really centralized system of government so long as communications had to go by road; for Tudor roads seldom allowed a horseman to average more than thirty miles a day. Inevitably the Tudors had to govern every district through

---

*Even the Royal Navy was left very largely to be built and run by what we should now call 'private enterprise'.

local men. Right up to the failure of the Northern rising of 1569 Northumberland 'knew no king but a Percy' and virtually paid no taxes; and once, when a Spanish treasure-ship was brought into Dartmouth, Ralegh had to be released from prison and sent to secure the Queen's share of the prize, as he alone could manage the wild Western men.

The squires and business men and lawyers, the men who did the work of government, the men on whose support the kings and queens depended, had to be cajoled or bluffed or bribed. They received their reward in many ways—in monastery lands, in patents of nobility, in appointments to high diplomatic or administrative posts, in licences to farm the monopoly of some manufactured or imported goods. Ralegh was no hero to the Londoners, who reviled him as the courtier who took a rake-off on their wines. It is significant that Mary never dared give back the abbey lands and that foreign policy was influenced, right up to the eve of the Armada, by the City's concern to keep open the door for its old trade with Spanish Flanders. The Conciliar Courts had been savage with the surviving feudal 'overmighty subjects', but the new aristocracy had to be given longer rope. The government would turn a blind eye when one squire, in his capacity as magistrate, allowed another to be under-assessed for subsidy taxation or to go unpunished for non-attendance at the parish church.

The importance of the squires and merchants was of course reflected in the coming of a new prestige to the Commons House of Parliament. We are apt to forget that this was not inevitable, that from the accession of Henry VII until the fall of Wolsey, Parliament was being used less and less. Perhaps only chance saved it from the atrophy which overtook the French Third Estate in the same period. When Cranmer wrote the Litany it was still natural to pray for King and Clergy, for Council, Nobility and Magistrates, but to omit the Commons. Chance, however, made the Commons a convenient ally for the King in his quarrel with the Pope; and once Parliament had been used to carry out a social and religious revolution there was no looking back. Henry VIII made concessions to the Commons and even encouraged their tentative requests for privilege. It was, of course, largely through the Commons that Elizabeth practised her wooings of the English people.

Part of the Tudor technique of government was never to let anything become too well defined. The wiser sovereigns knew how to blow hot and cold. Commons and squires were not allowed to move too fast or too far. Orators who claimed freedom of speech at inconvenient times or on inconvenient subjects might perish in the Tower. Nor were the new aristocracy encouraged to step over-hastily into dead men's shoes. There were two serious rebellions in favour of the old nobility and therefore the sovereign, discarding as it were from weakness, had to make it known that to be a nobleman was still important. Sir Philip Sidney was rebuked by the Queen for his impertinence as a mere knight in challenging the Earl of Oxford to a duel. Another knight, Sir Thomas Copley, got into trouble for styling himself 'nobilis Anglus' in a letter to the King of Spain.*

The same living from hand to mouth, the same search for equilibrium, the same shirking of final definition

---

*It is significant that no Tudor ruler considered flooding the House of Lords with new creations even when the Peers threatened opposition to a Government measure.

characterized Tudor religious policy. Perhaps it was a blessing that the English Reformation was so much governed by 'reason of state' and conducted in a spirit so worldly-wise and secular. The first and most drastic moves were rushed through in a decade by Henry VIII, from motives that were personal, political, constitutional and economic but not religious. The speed and skill of his tactics left the opposition standing. By the time conservatives realized that there had been a revolution it was already a vested interest too strong to be overthrown. Moreover, there was an English Reformation almost before there were any English Reformers. The earlier martyrs like Bilney, Frith and Barnes were orthodox on many points of doctrine; they were humanists or anti-clericals, indiscreet in their criticism, but nearer in their thought to Wyclif than to Luther. Even Latimer was hardly more than a Lollard when he was burnt. Edward VI's government had to import its Protestant intellectuals from abroad. The Open Bible took time to do its work and there was little popular Protestantism, as opposed to anti-clericalism, before the Fires of Smithfield lit their inextinguishable candle. It had been more the absence or the inefficiency of the clergy than their teaching which critics had attacked. The things that rankled had been the thirteen ecclesiastical offices held by Wolsey's bastard son while still a schoolboy or the holding of the see of Worcester by four consecutive absentee Italians, two of whom were murderers. Yet before the death of Henry VIII it was clear that doctrinal changes had to come. The people had been told that the Pope had no more authority in England. But the Pope held the keys of Heaven and Hell. Who then would let men into Heaven? Was the King so great that he could save their souls? Cranmer and others realized that the people must be taught a new doctrine in which salvation depended on a man's direct relationship with God. Under Mary many leading Reformers fled abroad and returned with the more rigid doctrinaire theology of Zürich or Geneva. Elizabeth found among them the only learned and able clergy upon whose loyalty she could rely. To appease them her new Church was given a Protestant theology. But, to satisfy the sentiments of ordinary people and to hoodwink foreign Catholic powers, a semi-Catholic liturgy was retained. This untidiness, adopted for purely worldly reasons, is sometimes called the Anglican *Via Media* and held to show the English genius for compromise. It was seen in a truer light by the Elizabethan Puritans, who recognized its political and almost cynical motives and maintained that the Protestant religion was true, not rather true, and was to be taken seriously, not rather seriously. Nevertheless, so strong by then was the tradition of relying on the Sovereign's command, even in religious matters, that for long no Puritan did anything but importune the Prince to be a 'Godly Prince'. Cartwright the Puritan leader was always saying 'Tarry for the Magistrate' and gave little colour to the view that 'no bishop' meant 'no king'. In a sense the Puritans also compromised. Some degree of peace and unity was secured and time was gained for the Prayer Book to exert its subtle mellowing influence. Anglicanism needed time to grow into something more than a purely political religion and could not do so before Hooker had given it an intellectual content.

Lowering the tension cost something in logic and perhaps in spiritual achievement. In all the wealth of Elizabethan poetry there are almost no religious lyrics of serious merit save those of the Jesuit martyr Southwell.

Yet much was gained. The violence had been got over quickly; there were no religious civil wars; and a real, if partial, approach was made towards toleration. In England alone the Reformation did not devour the Renaissance. England was fortunate in that the Renaissance reached her late when her Reformation was already half complete. Nowhere else did the Reformation draw so near to the New Learning. Nowhere else was it so easy for a great poet full of sweetness and light, like Spenser, to be a Puritan. The Reformers, too, brought into English life that high seriousness which saved the poets from being mere popinjays and the men of action from being mere 'toughs'. Without it England, in her new prosperity, might indeed have become a nation of shopkeepers and nothing more. The Puritan doctrine of the 'calling' has been charged with sanctifying money-grubbing. We forget that Milton felt 'called' to write an epic.

For a time the balance, variety and unity of national life under Elizabeth was reflected in the men themselves. Poets went on naval expeditions, politicians conducted chemical experiments, and Sir Humphrey Gilbert carried musicians and dancers on board his ship. Gabriel Harvey thought that Spenser should have learnt more astrology before writing poetry; and when Frobisher set sail to find the North-West Passage, the watchword and the countersign were two theological propositions—'Before the World was God' and 'After God came Christ his Son'.*

*It is recorded in the log of Captain William Keeling, of the East Indiaman *Dragon,* that his crew acted *Hamlet* in September 1607 when outward bound of Sierra Leone, and *Richard II* three weeks later. On March 31st, 1608, he wrote, 'I invited Captain Hawkins to a fish dinner and had *Hamlet* acted aboard me, which I permit to keep my people from idleness and unlawful games, or sleep'.

Dichotomies were not made between religion and politics, thought and action, reason and passion, literature and life, vision and reality. Prose could be gaudy, romantic and rhetorical; verse could be employed for a guide-book to England or a treatise upon husbandry. Verse indeed sold as readily as prose; and it helped poets and playwrights to know that rich and poor had some mythology in common, for most Englishmen had heard of Troilus and Cressida or Pyramus and Thisbe. Moreover, the people not only bought and sang the latest topical ballads; sometimes they spoke in poetry and made it for themselves, like the Irish peasants of a later age. Some of the best Border Ballads and many Nursery Rhymes are Tudor. The Elizabethans wrote at times in the most elaborate, tortuous conceits, and at other times with incomparable directness. When the author of the precious, mannered pastoral *Arcadia* discovered that his father's secretary had tapped his correspondence, he wrote: 'Few words are best. . . . If ever I know you to do so much as read any letter I write to my father, without his commandment, or my consent, I will thrust my dagger into you; and trust to it, for I speak it in earnest. In the mean time farewell'. Never, perhaps, in English history were the languages of speech and writing, and of thought and feeling so near together. The great and obvious proof is Tyndale's Bible. When Shakespeare's fellow-actors Heminge and Condell produced the First Folio in 1623 they recalled that 'his mind and hand went together: and what he thought, he uttered with that easiness, that we have scarce received from him a blot in his papers'.

Even in more material things a certain harmony and balance could be discerned—between wealth and poverty, town and country, sickness and health. Rising prices and debased coins, rack-renting and enclosure caused bewilderment and distress. But villeinage was over and, on the whole, both rich and poor were growing richer. The change from exporting raw wool to weaving cloth at home, together with a great spurt in coal-mining, inaugurated a miniature industrial revolution. The North Sea gave up its herrings and the Western Ocean was found to be not a barrier but a highway to undreamed-of sources of new wealth. By Elizabeth's time the housing, bedding, clothing and furniture of the poor had improved so notably that many of the better-off were calling for sumptuary legislation. The new houses had more chimneys and larger windows better glazed, although 'Hardwick Hall more window than wall' was an extreme case. With less smoke and more light men could see what lay about them. There followed a demand for more attractive household goods, for tapestry and needlework, and for pewter, glass or silver to replace the old wooden table-ware. Meat, however, was still eaten with knife and fingers, and the traveller Coryat saw his first fork in Italy. In clothing men were more fastidious. The rich became notorious for the expense and elaboration of their whimsical, unstable fashions. One man indeed sold sixty woods to pay for a pair of galligaskins. Even the middle classes spent sums out of all proportion to their incomes on garters, scarves or shoe-buckles. There were complaints that the classes could no longer be told apart; and Mistress Quickly once bought for Falstaff a dozen shirts, 'holland of eight shillings an ell'.

Although the water closet was invented by an Elizabethan courtier, sanitation continued to be 'un-American'. Dr. Andrew Boorde (c.1545) had good reason for saying 'Water is not wholesome, sole by it self, for

an English man'. Nor is it difficult to understand the
Tudor love of perfumes. Bacon and many others valued a
garden less for its colours than its smells. Yet improved
ventilation did something for public health; and
although Shakespeare's London had appalling visitations
of the plague, the sweating sickness (the peculiar scourge
of early Tudor England) had by then abated, and the
population had begun to rise a little. So had men's expec-
tation of life. Colet a hundred years before had lost twenty
brothers and sisters in infancy. By Shakespeare's time, perhaps, half a family might be expected to grow up, although
Claudio's sister could argue that her shame would only
bring him 'six or seven winters more'.

The English were not modest about their prowess or
their progress. In 1500 a Venetian, who said he had never
noticed an Englishman to be in love, observed nevertheless that 'the English are great lovers of themselves' and
think 'there is no other world but England'. Fifty years
later a Frenchman found the English given 'only to vanity
and ambition and merchandise'. Certainly the Tudor
Englishman walked the world and left it with swagger
and panache. We remember the jests and gestures that
More and Ralegh made upon the scaffold. There was
Rowland Taylor, coming to be burnt in his own parish
of Hadleigh and dismounting to 'set a frisk or twain as
men commonly do in dancing'; and, to the Sheriff's
'Master Doctor, how do you now?', replying: 'Never
better; for now I know I am almost at home, I lack not
past two stiles to go over and I am even at my Father's
house'. There was Sir Humphrey Gilbert, preferring 'the
wind of a vain report to the weight of his own life', sitting
with his book on the poop of his cockle-shell when the
'outrageous seas' broke 'short and high, pyramid-wise' and

calling out: 'We are as near heaven by sea as by land'. There was Ralegh leading the naval assault on Cadiz and answering the Spaniards' guns 'with the blare of a trumpet . . . disdaining to shoot one piece at any one or all of those esteemed dreadful monsters'. Above all there was Drake's game of bowls and the last fight of the *Revenge*.

Of all the rhetoric in *The Unfortunate Traveller* nothing could have pleased Elizabethan readers more than the 'insulting oration' of the criminal about to be broken on the wheel. 'Expect not of me a whining penitent slave, that shall do nothing but cry and say his prayers, and so be crushed in pieces. My body is little, but my mind is as great as a Giant's; the soul which is in me, is the very soul of Julius Caesar by reversion. My name is Cutwolf, neither better nor worse by occupation than a poor cobbler of Verona: cobblers are men and kings are no more.'

Nor did Tudor bombast prove hollow or fustian, for all its arrogance. Latimer's candle never was put out. Drake did sail, as he promised, in an English ship on the Pacific. Ralegh did give his Queen 'a better Indies than the King of Spain hath any'. What Hakluyt wrote, in words often quoted but still imperishable, was true: 'Which of the Kings of this land before her Majesty had their banners ever seen in the Caspian Sea? Which of them hath ever dealt with the Emperor of Persia as her Majesty hath done, and obtained for her merchants large and loving privileges? Who ever saw, before this regiment, an English Ligier in the stately porch of the Grand Signior at Constantinople? Who ever found English consuls and agents at Tripolis in Syria, at Aleppo, at Babylon, at Balsara, and, which is more, who ever heard of Englishmen at Goa before now? What English ship did heretofore ever anchor in the mighty river of Plate? Pass and repass the unpassable (in former opinion) strait of Magellan, range along the coast of Chile, Peru, and all the backside of Nova Hispania, further than any Christian ever passed, traverse the mighty breadth of the South Sea, land upon the Luzones in despite of the enemy, enter into alliance, amity and traffic with the Princes of the Moluccaes and the Isle of Java, double the famous Cape of Bona Speranza, arrive at the Isle of Santa Helena, and, last of all, return most richly laden with the commodities of China, as the subjects of this now flourishing monarchy have done.'

II

CONSTITUTIONAL DEVELOPMENT

J. HURSTFIELD

CONSTITUTIONAL history is the study of the possession and the employment of power. In other words, it is the history of government. During the sixteenth century, in Europe no less than in England, men were attempting to assess and explore the three vast changes which were taking place: the first was the religious revolution associated with the Reformation; the second, the economic revolution following upon the exploitation of the silver and gold mines of the New World and the rising price level; and the third, the geographical revolution, which was altering fundamentally the relationship of the European states with one another and with the rest of the world. In the process of adjusting themselves to these changes, some European countries found themselves embroiled in bitter internal struggles of a religious and political character. Faced with a dissolution of much that was old, men continued to search for stability in some new political order and yet the more they fought, the further did the goal of moderation and stability recede. In some countries, these ideals are now no nearer fulfilment than they were four centuries ago. Yet with the exception of certain phases, the sixteenth century in England saw the greatest measure of success in the approach to stability and moderation, the twin pillars upon which much of her constitutional structure was founded. If we search for a theme in the Tudor panorama, we may perhaps best trace it in the relationship between tradition and progress as revealed in the institutions of monarchy and parliament.

Political society, like nature, abhors a vacuum. This vacuum arose from the Wars of the Roses, which lasted for a generation during the second half of the fifteenth century. In the constitutional sense, the struggle revealed the weakness and incapacity of the baronage as such to exercise political power in a nation state. For other reasons, the merchants and the gentry lacked the experience and the organs to intervene with sufficient force in the struggle or to claim a share in government. The continuance of such an indeterminate situation not only threatened the wealth and the prospects of the country as a whole but jeopardized its very survival as a political entity. To fill the political vacuum, Henry VII (1485–1509) established the so-called Tudor despotism; the English monarchy resumed and extended the authority of government which had been disputed by its opponents during the greater part of the Middle Ages. The revived monarchy offered to the bulk of the population, and particularly to the politically conscious classes, the prospects of stability, unity and that security necessary for the utilization of the commercial opportunities which were awaiting them. Again, this development was not peculiar to this island. To a greater or less degree, the German princes, the French and Spanish kings and other rulers became the residuary legatees of political power within their territories and posed as safeguards against the ever-present threat of religious, political, economic and social anarchy. 'Le nouveau messie est le roi!' *M.*

But the monarchy of Henry VII differed in form and substance from that of the continental monarchies as well as from the absolutism, for example, of William the Conqueror in England. Henry's was an old institution but it was also a 'new' monarchy. It was old in that it harked back to the feudal prerogatives of the Crown as supreme overlord. Indeed, the highly successful efforts of Henry's ministers, Empson and Dudley, to revive the obsolescent feudal rights of the Crown comprised an important financial element of the government. It was old also in that it used the mediæval law courts, the mediæval officers and institutions such as sheriffs, escheators, justices of the peace and juries in the counties; and the Exchequer, the central financial machinery, was still functioning with its time-honoured methods at Westminster. It was old in that the monarchy continued to summon Parliament, in theory to seek its advice, in practice to collect additional funds. But it was new in that the Crown arranged the marriage between these ancient traditions and new concepts and new devices.

The judges continued to expound and enforce the practices of English common law, the law based upon the statutes of Parliament and the ancient custom of the land. But the Privy Council and its servants operated, during the Tudor period, through the prerogative courts of Star Chamber, Requests, High Commission and the delegated powers of the Councils of the North and of Wales. These courts were uninhibited by common law principles and were able to bring a speedy and inexorable

justice to those who could be brought within its jurisdiction. The Tudors, moreover, injected wherever practicable some measure of sixteenth-century efficiency into
the mediæval institutions of sheriff, escheator, justice of
the peace and jury; but they encountered resistance in
the process. Also, while the Exchequer continued to do its
mediæval arithmetic, the King's Chamber and the new
financial courts usurped many of its functions until the
Exchequer was reformed.

No less important, this was a time not simply of new
institutions but of new men. During the Middle Ages the
king had drawn his ministers from the clergy and the
feudal baronage, both of whom, and particularly the
baronage, had their own constitutional vested interests.
Nominally servants of the Crown, they had in fact shared
with him, and on occasion seized from him, whatever
power they could. Henry VII and the other Tudors drew
their ministers deliberately from humbler stock. Though
Wolsey, who died in 1530, may be regarded as the last
of the great ecclesiastic statesmen, his name, like those of
Empson, Dudley, Thomas Cromwell, Seymour, Cecil and
Walsingham, was never borne by the mediæval baronage.
These 'new men', who combined the functions of political
adviser and civil servant, were in time to develop vested
interests and traditions of their own, but for the present
they were personal servants of the Crown, conscientious
and loyal. In this way the king divested the baronage of
a very important feature of its mediæval power; and he
completed the rout with the statutes against maintenance
and livery, which prohibited the retention of private
armies. The use of the Privy Council by the Tudors as
the great executive and judicial organ of their will, with
its members drawn from their personal servants not their

WORKING MEN'S
COLLEGE
LIBRARY

HENRY VIII
after Hans Holbein's portrait at Althorp

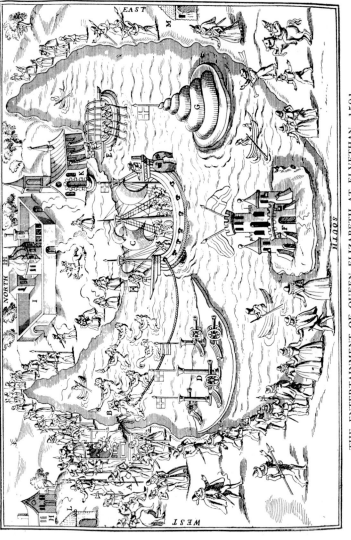

THE ENTERTAINMENT OF QUEEN ELIZABETH AT ELVETHAN, 1591

great feudal tenants, was of tremendous importance and clearly differentiated their system of government from what had gone before.

In Henry VII's reign we see the realization of some of the schemes briefly foreshadowed in the reign of his predecessor, Richard III (1483–1485), though in most of his work Henry showed himself to be a creative statesman. His son, Henry VIII (1509–1547) continued the process of strengthening the central government. In Thomas Cromwell, his outstanding minister from 1530 to 1540, Henry found an admirable instrument for his policy; and the concentration of political power in the royal hands was reinforced by the assumption of ecclesiastical supremacy as the result of the Reformation. The principal effects of the Reformation, which was carried through in England in the years 1529 to 1536, are considered elsewhere; but the immediate result was not simply to grant to Henry a primacy in ecclesiastical affairs but to lay at his feet the vast economic resources which the monasteries had stored up during the centuries.

In the reign of Henry VIII it may be said that Tudor absolutism reached its highest point; but it was never complete. There was Parliament to reckon with. Parliament still consisted of two Houses: the Lords, summoned by individual writ as members of the peerage and the Commons, (or as great ecclesiastics) elected to represent the boroughs and shires of England and Wales. Elections were, of course, neither by universal suffrage nor secret ballot. In the country the electorate consisted of freeholders of land worth forty shillings per annum; in the towns great variations occurred, the vote being sometimes restricted to the borough owners or a narrow oligarchy, sometimes extended to some or all house-

33

C

holders; and riot, force and fraud were not infrequent accompaniments of elections. The great lords and the tudor statesmen, through their connections, considerably influenced the composition of the House of Commons but the rising industrial and commercial classes, as well as the country gentlemen, were increasingly able to speak their mind in Parliament.

Moreover, to effect a religious revolution, Henry had employed Parliament both to lend legality to his sweeping claims and to reach out through Parliament to the informed opinion of the English people. The day was to dawn, however, under his successors, when Parliament, having gained the experience and tasted the pleasures of sharing political power with the king, would claim to be something more than his temporary assistant. Secondly, the great financial windfall which the Reformation brought was soon to be consumed by the heavy and expanding costs of government, and the time was coming when the monarchy was to call upon Parliament for greater financial aid than it had previously solicited, aid which would only be given on terms.

The success which attended the efforts of the first two Tudors to augment their power could not be made permanent in the short space of sixty years. Their system depended in large measure upon the strong personality of the king and the popular acquiescence in his rule. When such a firm hand was removed and the new monarch, Edward VI, ascended the throne at the age of ten, an inner weakness of Tudor power, in its dependence upon a strong personality, was revealed. First, from 1547 to 1549, Seymour, the Protector Somerset exercised the royal power until he was overthrown by faction; then, from 1549 to 1553, Northumberland wielded that authority until he overreached himself and claimed the throne on Edward's death for his son and daughter-in-law, the tragic Lady Jane Grey. Thus these new men tried to do what the mediæval barons had in their own day attempted, and what was to be attempted shortly afterwards during three decades of exhausting war in France: they sought not to overthrow the monarchy but to control it in their own interests. In England, it was not from this source that the real challenge to monarchical absolutism was to come.

Edward's half sister, Mary, was not a minor when she ascended the throne; no over-mighty minister arose to claim a preponderant share in government. But there were other defects. She was a woman, and no woman had previously ruled in England. She was a Catholic extremist and the fires of Smithfield which she kindled burned at the props of Tudor absolutism: at its moderation and popularity. Moreover, she married a Spaniard, Philip II; here was a union that might in time turn the country into an appanage of a continental despot. At the end of her reign the vituperative John Knox, with not only Mary in mind, had blown the first blast of his trumpet against the monstrous regiment of women—and was threatening to blow two blasts more! But Mary did not live long enough to undo the work of her father and grandfather. She damaged the prestige of monarchy and weakened its foundations but it was too well grounded in the needs of the time to dissolve in the growing volume of discontent.

Elizabeth, the last of the Tudors, inherited a throne whose power had been damaged alike by the weakness and intolerance shown during the last ten years. Her task was to restore it in the hearts of her people and in the centre of the constitutional arch. She believed that she could do it by firmness tempered with moderation. This moderation sounded the keynote of her rule. She turned the monarchy into a flexible instrument of government which adjusted itself to the fluid political situation of her long reign. She combined efficiency with tact and with an astonishing political acumen which out-witted and out-manœuvred her opponents at nearly every turn. To a degree not experienced by her predecessors, she had to face a growing volume of religious and political demands which must in time alter the character and struc-ture of the English polity. But she played her role with finesse and the efforts to circumscribe her power, which we must consider separately, met with little success in her own day. Her machinery of government, her law courts, her feudal resources, her control of policy were virtually intact when she died. But the problem of sovereignty was not solved, only masked. It was to emerge with renewed urgency under her Stuart successors, with a people more ambitious of power and a monarchy less shrewd in resisting it.

We have been considering hitherto the constitutional framework of England in terms of the power of the throne. But that is only one side of the picture. Even in its heyday the Tudor monarchy did not partake of the full measure of absolutism. It was in essence limited by two things in England: first, by the tradition of certain forms of government which could claim an ancestry as old as that of the king, and, secondly, by its need for money. It was these two limitations which were to sap the strength of the Tudor kingship and to force it, in a later century, to accept the conditions of a constitutional monarchy.

The first of these impediments to full supremacy has

already been noted. The common law of England, though it gave the king a central position and placed the judges as lions about the throne, had by the accretions of centuries embodied within its jurisdiction many safeguards for the subject. The common law was both enacted and traditional, or customary, law: the judges determined cases in the light of statutes and case law, that is, decisions made by their predecessors. Their verdicts could not normally be varied to meet the desires of the reigning monarch. The processes of trial were slow and cumbrous and the machinery was unwieldy, but these very defects served, in some respects, to shield the subjects against the intentions of a vigorous king or his overzealous servants. Moreover, a succession of distinguished lawyers in the Middle Ages, including Glanvill, Bracton and Fortescue, had written their commentaries upon the laws of England and, in the process, had laid down the principles which must govern the decisions of the King's judges. These principles, and the minutiæ of legal practice, had also been discussed for centuries in the Year Books and had been taught in the Inns of Court.

The new law courts of the Tudors eschewed the traditions of common law and based their judgements upon an adaptation of Roman civil law, law independent of English custom and looking directly to the will of the ruler to give validity and justice to its decrees. They could therefore bring their verdicts more closely into line with the contemporary needs of government and could determine causes logically and speedily. But though these law courts raised the status and power of the Crown, they did not invariably do so at the expense of all his subjects. Indeed, the Star Chamber was a valuable organ for putting down disorder in the countryside and, in addition, protected the people to some extent against the exactions and corruption of the king's officials. Many of his subjects flocked also to the Court of Requests where poor men's causes could be heard without the delay and expense of common law procedure. But there was a latent conflict between the two principal forms of law. The common law courts, jealous of their traditions no less than of their fees, would not tolerate indefinitely the expansion of the new courts at their expense. Here was a conflict of jurisdiction. There was also a fundamental conflict of outlook upon the state. This divergence was not to be brought to issue until the last of the Tudors had given place to the first of the Stuarts; but the quarrel between James I and Sir Edward Coke, the great common lawyer, was already implicit in the Tudor period. When James, following the civil law tenet, maintained that it was treason to affirm that the king was under the law of the land, Coke retorted with a quotation from Bracton that the king was 'sub deo et lege' (under God and the law). The survival of common law through the Tudor period limited the horizon of royal power.

There was a second, and in the end an insuperable, barrier to full absolutism, namely the disparity between royal expenditure and normal income. The revenue of the monarch in the sixteenth century came from various sources: his rents and profits as a great landowner; the feudal incidents such as escheats, reliefs and wardships as the supreme overlord; the fines and other receipts from his law courts; and the customs duties. With this income the king was expected to maintain himself and his household as well as pay the expenses of government at home and abroad. In mediæval language, the king was expected to 'live of his own'; these sources were sometimes called his 'ordinary' sources of revenue. A careful monarch such as Henry VII, exploiting his ordinary sources to the full and avoiding foreign adventures, might manage to live of his own and even leave a surplus to his successor. But apart from differences of personality, the later sovereigns found it impossible to achieve the same result. Government grew increasingly more expensive, a natural concomitant of the expansion of government itself. Ambassadors had to be maintained at foreign courts; armies, and sometimes allies, had to be paid and supplied with munitions; a growing body of officials at home, and some abroad, had to receive their fees, small though they often were. The normal sources of income of the Crown, particularly from land, were increasingly inadequate to meet their demands. The inadequacy was thus exacerbated by the inflationary waves which greatly reduced the purchasing power of the King's income arising from fixed rents. While expenditure rose real income shrank. When to these disadvantages a monarch added personal extravagance, as exemplified in Henry VIII, and was in any case obliged to live on his capital by the sale of land, he reduced thereby the annual income of his successors. War consumed a monarch's substance even more rapidly.

The ordinary sources were therefore not enough. The Crown could then try to meet its commitments in a number of ways: by loans, which could only postpone the day of reckoning and not radically alter the economic situation of the government; by imposing a disguised tax on industry and trade in the form of patents of monopoly, which would bring discontents in their train; or, finally, by going to Parliament and asking for the grant of special taxation. This form of income belonged to his 'extraordinary' sources and the term is significant. The accepted tradition, accepted alike by Crown and Parliament, was, in the first place, that taxation would be imposed only as an extraordinary measure and to meet an extraordinary situation; and secondly, such taxation could only be granted by Parliament on behalf of the king's subjects.

Parliament was thus summoned for one of three reasons; to mark the beginning of a new monarch's reign; to legislate, since it was recognized that the will of the king could not become law until it had passed through both Houses (royal proclamations never acquired the full force of legislation); and to grant him funds. The king could summon and dissolve Parliament at his will but his need for money was his Achilles heel and imposed a time limit upon his capacity to govern without Parliament. Once Parliament had assembled, and particularly when it was presented with a money bill, it might seize the opportunity for ventilating grievances and petitioning for redress. The time had not yet come when it would make its grants conditional upon such redress; but the parliamentary conflicts of the Stuart reigns cast their long shadows before them over the latter part of the Tudor era.

So Parliament during the sixteenth century, and particularly the House of Commons to which the government turned for supply, grew almost imperceptibly in strength. In Henry VII's reign Parliament met rarely and, in the last five years, not at all. In Elizabeth's reign it met more often; and it is again significant that there were only three parliaments in the first twenty-five years of her reign and six in the last twenty years. But the last twenty years were the years of war, in the Netherlands, in Ireland, in the Channel and on the high seas; and war cost money. The House of Commons was claiming, at first tentatively and then with rising courage, to express itself freely, as well as to ensure the freedom of its members from arrest and to advise the Crown about its foreign policy, its religious policy, the succession and other issues. Elizabeth firmly but gently resisted these intrusions upon her prerogatives but softened the blows with sweet words. 'Nay,' she said at the dissolution of 1567, 'it was never in my meaning [to break your liberties] but to stay you before you fell into the ditch.' How her words contrast with those of the learned James I, who reminded his faithful commons that when the Laecedemonians proposed legislation to their ruler they appeared before him with halters round their necks! In particular, since Parliament had been the instrument for effecting a reformation in Church life and government, Parliament claimed some voice in maintaining and interpreting that settlement. Thus Puritans, inside and outside of the House of Commons during Elizabeth's reign, focused upon Parliament their admonitions and tried to force upon the Crown a religious policy it was unwilling to adopt. As a personification of the new mood in political and ecclesiastical affairs, Peter Wentworth made the House of Commons the sounding-board for his doctrines, though he embarrassed his fellow members by the fervour and the intransigence of his views and, on one occasion, obliged them to silence him and commit him to the tower.

Thus it was not the Crown which was seeking the advice of Parliament but Parliament which was thrusting its advice upon the Crown. The famous debate on monopolies in 1601 brilliantly reveals the relationship of the protagonists. In the course of an angry debate, members denounced with bitterness and vehemence the strangling effects of monopolies upon trade and upon the social life of the community, and prepared to assume economic powers until now vested by implication in the authority of the Crown. As soon as the grave dangers, political and constitutional, inherent in such a situation were recognized by the queen, she graciously informed the commons in a message of sound judgement and good humour that the whole question would be re-examined. The Speaker, as the representative of the Commons, expressed gratitude and devotion for this act of 'princely justice'. Shortly afterwards the queen issued a proclamation against the abuses arising from patents. Thus the final definition of function of Crown and Parliament in this field was evaded and, in constitutional matters, no one really knew who had gained the shadow and who the substance. But great changes were brewing and, with the death of the queen, the English constitution entered upon a significant period of experiment and progress.

Every century is, in many respects, an age of transition. It reveals the adaptation of past institutions to contemporary and future needs. But the sixteenth century in England has a special reason for being so designated. It opened with the efforts of Henry VII to breathe new life into the mediæval apparatus of government and to employ men to aggrandize the ancient institution of kingship. It saw Henry VIII carry the process still further and assert his supremacy in ecclesiastical as well as in temporal affairs. In the short reigns of Edward VI and Mary the situation was too unstable to allow of any further progress in this direction; while the last forty years of the sixteenth century show that Elizabeth achieved on the whole a nice harmony of interests between what the Crown had won and what the new conditions required. But Parliament, a junior and intermittent partner of the Crown in the early part of the period, was beginning to emerge as a rival of its authority and jurisdiction. The situation during these later years was given only a temporary stability by England's struggle abroad and by the sensitive grasp which the queen retained both upon the system of government and the pulse of her people. When that grasp was withdrawn the changes inherent in the new age could no longer be delayed.

WORKING MEN'S COLLEGE LIBRARY

III

RELIGION

NORMAN SYKES

For though a day is never so longe,
At last the belles ringeth to evensonge.

A<small>ND</small> so with the coming of the sixteenth century the bells were ringing the vespers of the Middle Ages, in religion as in other spheres of human activity. For almost a thousand years since the coming of Augustine, these islands had been drawn within the orbit of Roman Christianity, sharing in greater or lesser degree during the various centuries in the religion, education, and civilization which Roman Christianity had given to Western Europe. At the apex of the vast organization of the mediæval Church stood the Roman papacy, the centre of unity and fount of law. For the genius for government which the Roman see inherited from the older empire of Rome found expression in the elaboration of an international system of canon law, administered and enforced in a hierarchy of courts Christian, from the archdeacon's court, which was the lowest in the scale, through the diocesan court of the bishop to the various provincial and metropolitan courts of the archbishop, and thence to the final authority in Rome itself. This canon law and its execution touched the life of the layman at many points; in all matters of moral conduct, in contracts of marriage and marriage itself, in the making and proving of wills, and in all cases involving a clerk as one of the parties. Also this elaborate organization needed constantly expanding resources of money; and the papacy was itself a prominent tax-gatherer, demanding regular payments in support of the vast army of clerks employed in the *curia Romana*. It was perhaps true that these two aspects of the mediæval papacy, its execution of ecclesiastical law which touched so nearly and often the lives of laymen and its need for more and more money which touched their pockets, played the most prominent part in the mediæval Englishman's conception of the papacy. It was natural that opposition was most easily provoked by them; for the canon law challenged the civil law and the common lawyers were jealous of the power and fees accruing to their rivals; and the financial demands of the papacy were a common ground of complaint. During the course of this thousand years also the Roman papacy had acquired estates and lands in Italy, and so had become a temporal kingdom, entering thereby (to the detriment of its universal spiritual claims) into the troubled conflicts of temporal politics, alliances and wars.

But of course and fundamentally the mediæval Church was the dispenser of sacraments, through which, as was believed, the grace of God was mediated to sinful humanity, and the teacher of those doctrines upon the acceptance of which depended also man's hope of salvation. Mediæval catholicism was thoroughly sacramental in character. Corresponding to human birth was the rebirth or regeneration of the child in Christian baptism. Parallel

to the growth of the child to adult age was the rite of
confirmation administered by the bishop. Just as the
physical body needed food to sustain its life, so the soul
was fed by the body and blood of Christ received in holy
communion; even as sickness of the body demanded the
skill of the doctor, so sins and sickness of the soul required
healing by auricular confession and absolution in the
sacrament of penance; at the solemn moment of the
union of man and woman in marriage, the Church blessed
that union by a religious rite; and at the end of life came
the anointing with holy oil in preparation for the soul's
journey, the solemn requiem mass for the soul of the
departed, and the interment of the body in the churchyard, whilst the procreation of children to continue the
human race had its spiritual counterpart in the rite of
ordination by which the ministry of the Church from age
to age was perpetuated. It is evident that many of these
sacraments could only be received once during the course
of an individual's life. But the chief sacrament, the Mass,
was of frequent celebration, and of vital importance in
the life of every man. If by a long-standing tradition he
received the element of consecrated bread only once each
year, at Easter and after his Lenten confession and absolution, yet the offering by the priest of the Mass as a
sacrifice for the sins of the living and the dead was a daily
duty, at which all the faithful were expected to assist
every Sunday and on greater holy days. During the later
Middle Ages, moreover, there had been a wide extension
of the custom of offering a series of masses for the delivery
from purgatory of the souls of the departed. The nature
and amount of preaching and teaching of the doctrines
of Christian faith given to the laity is difficult to ascertain.
It was the duty of the parish priest to teach his people to

46

repeat in English (for the Mass and other services of the Church were in Latin) the Lord's Prayer, the Hail Mary, and the Apostles' Creed, and to understand the faith expressed in this creed. Since the coming in the thirteenth century of the order of friars, the Franciscans and Dominicans, preaching had assumed new forms and a new popularity. The educated layman, moreover, would have a book of English prayers for use in his private devotion during his attendance at Mass. But for the uneducated person the opportunities of sharing with understanding in the worship of the Church were few. Nor was the standard of education of the average parish priest high. Notwithstanding, there is no evidence of general popular discontent with religion at the end of the fifteenth century. Indeed that century had seen the building of some of the finest English parish churches, such as those of East Anglia or the Cotswold district; but the close of the Middle Ages saw a steady decline in the popularity of the monastic life and in the numbers of inmates of monasteries and nunneries, whilst the friars had also declined sharply from their original poverty and self-sacrifice. In many ways the mediæval Church needed reform; and it was its chief misfortune that neither its head, the papacy, nor the generality of its leaders, the episcopate, were adequately equipped to deal with the reform of abuses or the challenge of new religious ideas. The papacy was largely concerned with its political problems in Italy and its financial needs; and the majority of bishops were royal nominees, promoted in recompense for their service to the king and state rather than for theological learning or devotion to the spiritual duties of their office. Accordingly it was not surprising that when the conflict between pope and king came to a head in

England, the great majority of the English bishops followed the royal rather than the papal cause.

The incident which provoked the storm was the desire of Henry VIII to secure the annulment of the papal dispensation by which he had been allowed to marry Catherine of Aragon; but this was the occasion, not the cause of the English reformation. Moreover the history of that reformation suffered various fluctuations of fortune; under Henry VIII it was limited generally to the repudiation of the pope's authority with little change in doctrine or forms of worship; under Edward VI an advance was made towards Protestant doctrine and worship, of which the First and Second Edwardine Prayer Books and the Forty-two Articles of Religion were the expression; under Mary the pendulum swung back to the complete restoration of papal power; and it was not until the long reign of Elizabeth that the reformation settlement in the Church of England won a slow but growing stability. What were the chief characteristics of this Anglican reformation?

First, all vestiges of papal authority were abolished in finance, in the canon law, and in the administration of the Church. From this radical reform the Crown was the chief beneficiary. Henry VIII assumed the title of Supreme Head of the Church of England, and Elizabeth accepted the modified title of Supreme Governor; but this designation was carefully explained to cover only power and authority of jurisdiction, and not to involve any claim to spiritual status or powers. Many of the financial dues formerly paid to Rome went into the royal pocket, until Queen Anne surrendered these first-fruits and tenths for the benefit of poor incumbents. The canon law continued in force and operation except in so far as it was contrary to the statutes of the realm, to the royal prerogative and the customs of the realm; but the final court of appeal was now the King in Chancery. Moreover the Crown could delegate the exercise of its jurisdiction over the Church to commissioners. The legislative bodies of the Church, the two Convocations of Canterbury and York, were only allowed to enact new canons with the express authority and sanction of the king. But the government and administration of the Church continued in the hands of archbishops, bishops and their subordinates; and no important change was made in the internal organization of the Church, save where necessitated by the abolition of the papal supremacy. Bishops were nominated by the Crown, elected by the cathedral chapter of their see, and consecrated by three bishops; and in turn they ordained the inferior clergy, the priests and deacons.

In the sphere of public worship the revolutionary step was taken of requiring all services to be in the English tongue. The Prayer Books of Edward VI and the Elizabethan Prayer Book of 1559 (which was in effect the Second Edwardine Prayer Book of 1552 with a few changes) embodied this new principle that the divine service of the Church should be a *common* worship, in which all subjects could join, and of which they possessed the full and exact forms in their English prayer books. The doctrinal standards of the Church were defined by the Prayer Book and by the Thirty-Nine Articles of Religion; the latter stating the Anglican position on controversial issues in language of studied moderation and comprehensive character. Perhaps the meaning of the reformation was brought home to the ordinary layman most by two factors; the placing of an English Bible, containing a translation of all the books of the Old and New Testaments in every parish church, for use both in the public services of the congregation and in private reading; and the outward changes in the parish church. As the reign of Elizabeth advanced the parish churches came to reflect the changes in religion. In place of the former images and mural paintings, instead of the mediæval ornaments of the church and the vestments of the clergy, instead of the stone altars and shrines, came a general whitewashing of the walls, the writing over the east end of the Lord's Prayer, the Ten Commandments, and the Apostles' Creed in English, the provision of wooden holy tables for the Lord's Supper, and the wearing of the white surplice by the minister in public worship; whilst on Sundays divine service consisted of Morning Prayer with the Ante-Communion, except on those days when the laity received the Communion, which they received in both bread and wine of course. It was not to be expected that there would be any speedy advance in the standard of education of the clergy; and during the reign of Elizabeth a great many ministers were not licensed to preach, and so their congregations had to be contented with the reading of the official *Homilies* instead of a sermon. Attendance at church on Sundays was enforced by the infliction of a money fine.

Unfortunately also many of the clergy who were able to preach were dissatisfied with the organization and worship of the Church, and were anxious to reform it more thoroughly. For in Scotland the reformation had been more radical, and had resulted in the substitution of a presbyterian form of Church government for episcopacy and the use in public worship of a form modelled on that of Calvin at Geneva. The more zealous Puritans in England wished to introduce this further reformation into the Church of England; and the queen and bishops had to struggle hard both against attempts in the House of Commons to introduce changes into the Church, and against local experiments towards the introduction of the presbyterian system of organization and discipline by incumbents and laymen who were sympathetic to the Calvanist regime. This presbyterianizing party had strong support in the Privy Council itself. But as it became evident that Elizabeth and her bishops would not give way, and that the royal power could stifle all attempts in parliament to proceed to 'the reform of the reformation', a new and more aggressive form of dissent came to the fore, in the shape of Independency. Against the episcopalian and presbyterian ideal of a national Church, in which churchmanship was coextensive with citizenship, independency upheld the ideal of a 'gathered' Church, consisting only of the 'elect' whom God had called out of the midst of this naughty world to be His Church or people. In this conception, the local Church was completely sovereign, autonomous and independent; in fact the congregation is the Church; all its members are 'churchmen', and the difference between minister and people is one of function not of order. The pastor is called and commissioned by the local congregation; and needs no other ordination than that so given. Neither ordination by fellow-presbyters nor by a bishop is needful. Moreover in the gathered Church the civil magistracy, from the queen downwards, can have no authority nor concern, save as individual members of the Church, subject to the same discipline and censure as all other members. In accordance with these principles separatist Churches or congregations outside the Established Church were formed; whilst the Presbyterian-

Puritans mainly remained within that Church, hoping for its ultimate remodelling by their patience in 'tarrying for the magistrate'.

On the other side there were also, since the papal bull excommunicating Elizabeth, Roman Catholic Recusants who refused attendance at the services of the Established Church and thereby constituted another element of dissent. During the uneasy first decade of Elizabeth's reign there had been general conformity on the part of malcontents, both Puritan and Papist; but with the restored self-confidence of the Roman Church, thanks to the work of the Council of Trent and the zeal of the Jesuit order, the movement of the counter-reformation was gathering momentum, and with the issue of the bull *Regnans in excelsis* in 1570 the period of conformity and compromise for the pope's followers in England was ended. Henceforth they were to be in open opposition; and their opposition was inevitably extended from the purely religious to the definitely political sphere by the clause in the bull which absolved Elizabeth's subjects from their civil allegiance to her as sovereign. Recusants, therefore, were doubly suspect; and with the rising toll of plots against the life of Elizabeth, of foreign conspiracies centring in Mary, Queen of Scots, and of plans for the invasion of England, the utmost severities of the law were invoked against Recusants. No subject was put to death for religion before 1570; but afterwards the number of martyrs, both Puritan and Recusant, steadily mounted. In many cases affecting Recusants the line between religious dissent and political treason was difficult to discern; in the case of Puritan victims there was no question of political disloyalty, and their sufferings were for conscience sake, and their deaths a sad commentary on the divisive effects of religious dissension. Their names are remembered as the proto-martyrs for Independency.

Behind this conflict with Recusant and Puritan, the Elizabethan Church was stabilizing its position, developing its traditions of belief, worship and practice, and winning a sure place in the affections of its adherents by other and nobler weapons than those of judicial process and sentence. At the beginning of Elizabeth's reign the *Apologia pro Ecclesia Anglicana* by John Jewel (1522-1571) had laid down the main lines of Anglican defence against the attacks of Rome, by asserting the fundamental continuity of the Elizabethan settlement in matters of faith, ministry, and worship with the primitive Church, by appealing from contemporary Rome to the tradition of the first five centuries of the Church, by emphasis on the authority of Scripture, and by insisting that reform was restoration not revolution. Towards the end of the century *Of the Laws of Ecclesiastical Polity* by Richard Hooker (1554-1600) took up the challenge of the Puritans, and, in what has become a classic exposition of Anglican principles, set forth their triple basis in Scripture, tradition, and reason. This comprehensive conception of the nature and basis of the authority of the Church of England was the most characteristic feature of Hooker's apologetic. Refusing to be tied on the one hand by the Puritan demand for positive precept and evidence in Holy Scripture for all the regulations, rites and ceremonies of the Church, on the other side he repudiated the equality between ecclesiastical tradition and the Bible which the Council of Trent had accepted. Moreover, he recognized that there were many regions of human thought and activity, including some provinces of religion and Church order themselves, where Scripture was either silent or ambiguous in its evidence. In this wide territory, Hooker claimed the right of reason to its own exercise of authority and decision, and also the right of Churches to differ from each other in their rules and practice. In the light of Hooker's great work, what might otherwise have seemed to be mere compromise or even political expediency in the Church of England may be interpreted as a wise and just comprehensiveness; aiming in matters secondary to include a wide diversity of belief and custom, and keeping careful watch to see that the province of those fundamental points of Christian faith upon which unity and agreement were essential, was not enlarged by the inclusion of things indifferent. Of course on the political side Hooker was a firm defender of the royal supremacy, and of the sixteenth-century ideal of the identity of churchmanship and citizenship. He desired the Church of England to be in fact as well as in aspiration a national Church, within which, thanks to its comprehensiveness, its distinction between fundamentals and things accessory, and its allowance of differences of opinion and usage in the latter, all citizens might be included. There can be no doubt that his apologetic established the principles of the religious and theological position of the *Ecclesia Anglicana;* and it was largely thanks to the work in the sixteenth century of Thomas Cranmer (1489–1556), Matthew Parker (1504–1575), John Jewel, and Richard Hooker that the Anglican tradition was developed and struck such deep roots as not to be overthrown even by all the convulsions, ecclesiastical and political, of the seventeenth century and of the Stuart monarchy. 'By the goodness of Almighty God and His servant Elizabeth, we are': such was the grateful tribute of Hooker to the queen. But her defence of the Church against external assault would have been of little effect without its religious appeal which was making its way slowly and steadily thanks to the Book of Common Prayer, the English Bible, and the literary defences of Jewel and Hooker.

IV

TOWN LIFE AND COMMERCE

S. T. BINDOFF

To-day we are a nation of townsfolk. Three-fifths of us live in communities of fifty thousand or upwards. By contrast, four centuries ago the vast majority of Englishmen lived in the country. Statistics are largely lacking, but the town-population did not perhaps amount to more than one-tenth of the whole. The urban concentrations which accounted for this small fraction of that small population were, in consequence, minute in comparison with those to which we are accustomed. With the exception of London, which then as now was in a class by itself, there was probably no Tudor town with more than 20,000 inhabitants and less than a dozen with 6,000 or more. The 'typical' city, borough or market-town was a place of two or three thousand people, that is to say, it matched in size such insignificant towns as Arundel or Blandford, Helston or Honiton, Shaftesbury or Southwold, Wallingford or Wilton in our own day. The three 'giants' among these pygmies were Bristol, Norwich and York, which may alone have reached the five-figure mark, while towering above them all there stood the capital, which early in the century topped 100,000 and before it was out had passed a quarter of a million. If London had yet to achieve its present position of holding one-fifth of the nation, it was, in comparison with other English towns, even more pre-eminent than it is to-day.

The smallness of the average Tudor town was one of the determining factors in its appearance. The physical antithesis between 'town' and 'country' which we take for granted was then much less apparent; indeed, the word 'town' itself had not yet been narrowed to its present connotation, and Tudor statutes against the 'decay of towns' were often in fact measures against the depopulation of the countryside. Not only did every part of a town then enjoy that proximity to the country which is now the privilege of its periphery, so that a man might quickly walk from the heart of the town to the heart of the country, but the transition from the one to the other was far from abrupt. Even towns which had retained that most unmistakable of urban boundaries, an enclosing wall, had begun to develop a suburban fringe outside it, while the area enclosed still wore, save perhaps at its very centre, a semi-rural air. In modern terminology, the Tudor town had a low building-density. Its houses and shops were set among fields, gardens and orchards, while in the many cases where towns were sited upon rivers, the meadows since drained and built over then for the most part lay open. It was partly a cause, partly an effect, of this pervading rusticity that the sixteenth-century townsman remained far closer to the soil than his twentieth-century successor, and that his livelihood came, not merely from making and selling, but also from growing and rearing. Generally speaking, the larger the town, the greater its concentration upon industry and trade, and the slighter its participation in agriculture. But at least in the early Tudor period no town had yet carried this specialization to the point where it could easily dispense with its plots and fields. This was the reason why the enclosure movement affected the towns as well as the countryside of Tudor England. Their rights of common on the town fields were hardly less dear to its inhabitants than were the common rights of villagers. Coventry waged a long struggle against the enclosure of its Lammas fields, and the evidence collected by the commissioners of 1548 about enclosure in Cambridge explains why some of that town's 5,000 inhabitants were disposed to make common cause with the rebellious peasants of the surrounding countryside. Even Londoners were affected by enclosure, although the burden of their protest was the more familiar one of the loss of open spaces for recreation. One morning in 1514 a concourse of the city's youth went out and threw down the hedges enclosing their traditional playground, the fields towards Islington, Hoxton and Shoreditch.

Yet for all their resemblance to overgrown villages the towns of Tudor England gave rise to problems which taxed the resources of the age. A city-father of the period might well have anticipated and adapted the lines of our own Poet Laureate:

> To get our whole town out of bed
> And washed, and dressed, and warmed, and fed,
> To work—and back to bed again
> Believe me, friend, costs worlds of pain.

The town's greatest and most constant preoccupation was its food supply. The adjacent, and if necessary the more distant countryside had to be persuaded to 'serve the market' and the victualling trades to distribute the food within the town at a reasonable price and in an edible condition. This involved a degree of municipal control which challenges comparison with the work of our own Local Food Offices, and in time of dearth gave rise to investigations and calculations which have a familiar ring. It was a food-crisis which prompted the magistrates of Coventry to undertake, in 1520, what was probably the first municipal census. It told them—and us—that there were 6,601 mouths to be fed in the town. And even if grain were available, it was not always easy to enforce the regulations, including the weight and price of the loaf, designed to ensure that everyone got his share. In 1557 the city of Chester was faced with a strike of its bakers, who refused to abide by the price prescribed, and the mayor was forced to take drastic action to maintain supplies. There was, indeed, hardly any limit to what a town might have to do to ward off the danger of famine. The problems of water supply, drainage and sanitation were less acute only because contemporaries were less aware of them. Our forefathers used much less water than we do; neither domestic nor industrial consumption approached the levels of our own day. But water they had to have, and the more closely they were congregated together the more difficult they found it to get. The mediæval pioneers of water supply were the great religious houses, and when these were dissolved by Henry VIII the towns which had grown up around them often took over and adapted their systems. Water was brought into towns from nearby springs or catchment areas by open channels (leats) or, less often, by pipes. Some of these leats survive to this day; the Tiverton leat is still the object of a septennial perambulation, and the channel at Plymouth known as Drake's Leat commemorates the installation of a new supply there, with the great seaman's co-operation, in 1591. Most town dwellers drew their water direct from the cisterns or conduits into which the leats discharged, but the practice of piping into houses (in return for the payment of a water rate) had become fairly common by the end of the century. The precautions taken to prevent the fouling of the water were primitive enough by modern standards, but since little or no water was drunk they were less inadequate than they would be in our own water-drinking society. All the same, the risk of infected water must be regarded as one of the factors conducing to the unhealthiness of town life. So must the defective provision for the disposal of garbage and sewage. It is difficult for us to conceive of a town of any size without water closets or main drainage, but Tudor towns did without either. At the opening of the century many of them were even doing without any organized removal of refuse, and their only scavengers were the flocks of kites and ravens whose presence in London and elsewhere was remarked upon by foreign visitors. In the course of the century, however, most towns improved upon this, and the municipal dustcart became a recognized institution. Bye-laws also dealt with such 'nuisances' as tanneries, slaughter-houses and pigsties. Even so, the standard of sanitation achieved cannot have been high, and were any of us transported back into the Chester or Norwich of 400 years ago we should doubtless find it a sufficiently dirty and malodorous town, especially if our visit happened to fall on market day.

But it is certain that the London of the period would leave a far worse impression. For London was twenty or thirty such towns rolled into one, and all its problems were of proportionate magnitude. Its food supply the capital drew chiefly from the home counties, but it was ever pushing the tentacles of its victualling organism farther afield, and by the close of the century corn and cattle were reaching the London markets from remote parts of the country. This was a development of far-reaching consequence. For if its ability to feed itself from an ever-widening area was London's best safeguard against famine, the 'metropolitan' corn market thus created was also to prove England's best prophylactic against the local dearths which continued to afflict such countries as France and Spain, where no such unifying force was at work. But during the sixteenth century the capital's food supply only just kept pace with its population, and vigorous action was often called for to overcome temporary crises. The Tudor monarchs needed no reminder that this great concentration of manpower, which was one of their chief assets so long as it remained amenable and loyal, could easily, under the pressure of hunger, be transformed into a serious liability, and they were always ready to support the city authorities in their efforts to keep that vast stomach filled. The London water supply was also the object of public solicitude. Between 1400 and 1563 twelve conduits were added to the system. (The name of one of them, reconstructed by William Lambe, a leading citizen and benefactor, in the mid-sixteenth century, is preserved in Lamb's Conduit Street, Bloomsbury.) There was also a corps of professional water-carriers, who, when they formed themselves into a Company, numbered, it is said, no less than 4,000. Thames water, impure as it must have been owing to the free use made of the river as a sewer, was much in demand, and in 1582 the Dutchman Peter Morice installed at London Bridge the apparatus for raising it to city-level which was to remain there until the bridge itself was demolished in 1822. But the modern history of London's water supply really begins in 1609, when Hugh Myddleton began to construct the famous New River which was to bring water from 38 miles away, and whose terminal point, New River Head, Islington, is still the headquarters of the Metropolitan Water Board. It was about the same time that London began to solve its third great supply problem, that of fuel, by substituting coal for wood. The near-exhaustion of the country's timber had rendered wood prohibitively expensive, and both in industry and in the homes of the people the adoption of coal averted a fuel famine. The bringing of 'sea coal' from Newcastle soon developed into a gigantic trade, and to the other impurities of the London atmosphere there was added the smoke from thousands of chimneys. Is it simply a coincidence that the word 'fog' first came into use about this time?

The trinity of food, water and fuel which ensured life and growth to London was insufficient to ensure longevity to Londoners. Not for another two centuries was the population of the capital to show any significant natural increase; until that time it was to continue to grow almost solely through immigration from the provinces and from overseas. We shall, indeed, scarcely be exaggerating if we say that London allured some of the best of the nation's manhood and womanhood and then killed them. The most spectacular—though not perhaps the most deadly—agent in this grim process was the plague. While the countryside and the provincial towns were (except when infected from London) largely immune from attack,

London paid the penalty of its size and its pre-eminence as a port by suffering regular and frequent visitations. We know now (as contemporaries did not) that plague is a rat-and-flea-borne infection, and that it was their rat-infested homes and workplaces and their flea-ridden garments and furnishings which together exposed Londoners to its ravages. The measures taken against plague by officials and physicians, serviceable as they were in limiting outbreaks, were wholly ineffectual in preventing them, and almost every generation of Londoners made sacrifice to the prevailing ignorance and the prevailing filth. The capital was eventually to be delivered from these recurrent ordeals by way of another—ordeal by fire. Tudor towns, with their preponderance of thatched roofs and their ill-constructed and ill-swept chimneys, lived in constant peril from fire, and one after another they suffered disastrous conflagrations. Here again, town authorities did what they could. They provided fire-fighting equipment, and some went so far as to forbid thatching. But the tempo of their counter-measures seldom matched that of the enemy, and the experience of Tiverton, where in 1598 there leapt out of a frying-pan a fire which destroyed 500 houses and killed 50 people, typified the suddenness and magnitude of these catastrophies.

Officially, an outbreak of plague or fire was, in the literal meaning of the words, an 'act of God' to punish human wickedness. But privately it must often have been regarded as the last blow of a malignant fate against a community which already had enough trouble to keep its place in a changing world. For in the life of most English towns the Tudor period was to prove an anxious and disappointing time. They had arisen in the Middle

Ages chiefly as centres of trade and industry, and the
Tudors certainly took it for granted that these should
remain the principal spheres of urban activity. Unfortunately, in their day—and partly in consequence of their
rule—powerful forces were at work to obliterate the
traditional division of function between town and
countryside, and nothing that either the Tudors or the
towns themselves did could protect them from the effects.
Industry then meant, first and foremost, the manufacture
of cloth. The spinning of yarn and the weaving of cloth
were occupations almost as widespread as the tilling of
the soil, and there can have been few peasant families
which did not find seasonal or part-time employment in
them. But for some centuries England had been building
up a large-scale cloth industry which served both the
home and the foreign market. Originally located in
towns, the industry had early shown a tendency to
migrate into the countryside, and this movement was in
full swing under the Tudors, while at the same time
newer industries like mining and alum-making were
also converting agricultural into industrial areas. Thus,
instead of their ideal economy of towns which flourished
by their manufactures and a countryside which flourished
by its agriculture, the Tudors saw an urban cloth industry
in full decline and a rural one expanding. It was in more
than one way a disturbing picture. Among all their subjects the Tudors looked in the first place to townsmen to
support their regime, and a movement which undermined the economic basis of urban strength was bound
to cause them alarm. Again, the Tudors were firm
believers in the virtue of regulation, and no industry
invited regulation so much as the woollen industry, the
staple industry of the realm and the foundation of its

export trade. The detailed code which they had in view—controlling the size, quality and price of cloth, the training of those who made it, and the conditions under which it was made—was much easier to apply in towns, where municipal and guild authorities stood ready to enforce it, than in an industry scattered over miles of countryside. Finally, the Tudors were led to question whether a cloth industry as massive and sprawling as that which developed under their rule did not conduce to national weakness rather than to national strength. Exposed to the continual fluctuations of the European-wide market which it served, the cloth industry appeared, alike in its booms and its depressions, a disturbing element in the national economic and social order. Flourishing, it encouraged enclosure and dislocated the rural structure; languishing, it created mass unemployment and bred discontent. Thus, when from the middle of the century the Tudors set about trying to reduce the industry to more manageable proportions, they thought instinctively in terms of confining it once again to the towns, and in a series of statutes and proclamations they sought to restore the 'good old order'. But this was to battle with the flood tide of economic change, and against that even Tudor strength and experience were of little avail. The rural centres of industry continued to forge ahead—and in the process to lay the foundations of the great industrial towns of modern England—while the older urban centres declined into industrial insignificance.

The same influences which were changing the country's industrial pattern were producing similar effects upon its trade. The two institutions through which the exchange of goods had been mainly effected during the later Middle Ages were the market and the fair. The

65

market had served the commercial needs of each district, the fair had been the agency of trade upon a national and international scale. The weekly market, of which every town had at least one, underwent relatively little change under the Tudors, and indeed it was to survive intact under Stuarts and Hanoverians and only to disintegrate in the welter of change which we call the Industrial Revolution. At the market, town and country met to exchange their wares: clothes, implements and luxury articles exchanged for crops, livestock and industrial raw materials. The clientele was predominantly local—although the bounds of the area to be served gave rise to interminable wrangling—and the market thus never lost sight completely of the mediæval ideal of direct contact between producer and consumer. But just as the market had earlier needed to be supplemented by the fair, so now the exchange of goods between different parts of England, and between England and abroad, was increasingly performed by a different set of agencies. The mediæval fairs lived on, and some of them, like Stourbridge Fair at Cambridge, remained important dates in the businessman's calendar. There were the specialized fairs, too, like the herring fair at Great Yarmouth and the horse fairs in the North, which were still the peaks of their particular trades. But most fairs were fast shedding their economic significance and becoming simply occasions of feasting and merry-making. The greatest of these junketings, Bartholomew Fair in London, which had grown up around the annual delivery of cloth by the country manufacturers to the Merchant Adventurers, had already established itself as the capital's biggest and most riotous holiday.

The chief agent in the decline of the fair, and at the

same time its principal legatee, was the middleman. Although he bore a different name—badger, broker, chapman, factor were some of them—in almost every branch of trade which he entered, the function of the middleman was everywhere the same—to link buyers and sellers whom time or distance prevented from doing business with each other save through his intermediary. Such was the office of the corn badger, who bought up grain at farms or in local markets for transmission to London or overseas; of the cloth factor, who made the round of the clothing districts taking cloth from small producers for delivery to wholesale merchants; of the coal and timber dealers, who bought in larger and sold in smaller quantities. It was this distributive network which alone made possible progressive regional specialization in both agriculture and industry, and which out of growing local diversity created growing national unity. But, inevitable and indispensable as he was, the middleman was universally condemned. Adding nothing, so it was thought, to the value of the goods which passed through his hands, the middleman lived by selling dearer than he bought, and his gain was another's loss. He was especially obnoxious to the provincial townsman, whose cherished local monopoly he was continually infringing by his long-range operations. He took the whole country, if not the whole world, for his province, and to the economics of the parish pump he opposed the wider, if equally self-interested, creed of the mercantile state.

To the rule that the industrial and commercial changes of the sixteenth century were alike unfavourable to towns there remains one tremendous exception. Under the Tudors London not only held its own as a manufacturing centre, but blossomed forth as a commercial metropolis.

Besides its supremacy in the production of all those articles of luxury and fashion for which a rising standard of living was continually widening the market, London also kept or acquired the lead in a number of important industries such as silk-weaving, brewing, soap-boiling, sugar-refining and tanning. It was these trades which largely supported the growing population of the industrial belt, from Clerkenwell to Whitechapel, north and east of the walled city, and which already before the end of the century had started to flow across to the south bank of the river. Alien immigrants, such as the silk-weavers from France and the Netherlands, were notable recruits to London's industrial population. But it was not industry, but commerce, which was to be the mistress of the city's economic destiny. As we have already seen, the satisfaction of London's own needs, in food, fuel and raw materials, called into being a distributive organism of increasing size and complexity, whose ramifications were soon covering a large part of the country. It was the trade thus generated which made up the bulk of the business done at the London markets. Corn, meal, malt, fish, meat, poultry, hay, leather, coal, all had their appropriate markets, which were generally located on the fringe of the densely built-up area. (The fact that one of the hay-markets was to give its name to a thoroughfare in the heart of the modern West End reminds us how modest an area that was.) The same mechanism which brought these prime necessities to London also served to carry them into other parts of the country. For the capital, besides being the greatest consumer of such things, became steadily more important as a national distributing centre for them. The surplus left over after its own needs were satisfied was despatched either further inland or abroad; goods brought in by sea, like fish and coal, moved on up the Thames and its tributaries, while those brought in by river and road went downstream to join the coastal or export trade. And with them went all the things which Londoners themselves made or processed—silks and satins, ornaments and jewellery, paper and books, sugar, spices, soap and beer.

With them, too, went the great volume of goods which were moving into or out of the country through the port of London. In no sphere was the uniqueness of London more evident than in foreign trade. Under the Tudors the capital came to handle some four-fifths of the country's overseas trade. It was the headquarters of all the great foreign trading companies, from the Merchant Adventurers at the beginning to the East India Company at the end of the century, and there were few branches of foreign trade in which it did not outstrip all competitors. To London itself this achievement brought, along with unrivalled wealth and power, a tightening of the hold of commercial capital and of the commercial outlook over its business life; its major industries fell into dependence upon the trading elements represented by the Livery Companies, and within the commercial world itself the requirements and standards of overseas trade increasingly dictated policy. On London's erstwhile rivals, the provincial ports, the situation imposed a struggle to preserve what they could of their dwindling prosperity; only ports like Bristol in the West or Newcastle in the North, whose position and independent trading connections still offered them scope for development, remained relatively immune. Finally, to the older urban centres of industry the grip of London appeared to mean their own slow strangulation. For it was the demands of London which above all encouraged the growth of rural industry, and it was London which in return flooded the country with imported wares. The resulting struggle between, on the one hand, the provincial towns, and on the other, the industrialized countryside backed by the wealth and influence of London, constitutes one of the leading themes of Tudor economic history and accounts for a good deal of Tudor economic legislation. It also explains the jealousy and suspicion with which the provinces eyed the capital, the root of their own troubles and, as they believed, the enemy of national welfare.

But provincial heads had much more to do than to shake in gloom, and although nothing seemed to work for the best in their far from best of all worlds the townsmen of Tudor England went on cultivating their gardens. Town magistrates renewed their charters, acquiring new privileges and evading old restrictions. They enlarged their boundaries, took over long-coveted properties (especially the ecclesiastical windfalls brought down by the great storm of the Reformation), and multiplied public amenities. They paved, swept and lighted their streets, and built or refurbished their town halls, market crosses, hospitals, almshouses and lock-ups. They grappled as best they could with the rising problems of unemployment, poverty, old age and sickness. They financed this growing range of public services from rates and contributions, and when these fell short they sold admissions to citizenship or floated loans. They studiously cultivated the magnates and courtiers who came more and more to monopolize their stewardships and recorderships and their representation in Parliament; and from time to time there fell to them the supreme (and ruinously expensive) honour of a royal visit. If their outlook and standards remained instinctively parochial, they did not fail, as they came to know more about the 'foreigners' who lived a county or two away, to improve their criteria of municipal efficiency and dignity, and hand in hand with a growing national patriotism they stimulated and shared in a fuller civic pride. While, therefore, it is true that with a handful of exceptions the towns of Tudor England belonged to the past, and that the future was not to lie with them, that future, now become the present, may yet look back with gratitude upon an urban culture which enshrined so much that was honest and pleasing and which is itself now enshrined in such monuments of rare beauty as Chipping Campden and Burford.

WORKING MEN'S COLLEGE
LIBRARY

V

COUNTRY LIFE AND ECONOMICS

V. M. WADSWORTH

UNDER the princely and paternal despotism of the
Tudors, England changed from a system designed
primarily for self-sufficiency to one under which
international trade was fostered, a new seapower built up,
and the immigration of foreigners who might found new
industries was encouraged. Under what became known as
the mercantile system, England grew prosperous, and laid
the foundations of her industrial future. But as yet agriculture was still the main occupation of her people. For
centuries wool had formed the staple export of the nation,
and, acknowledged at this time as the best in Europe,
was the real source of the country's wealth. Indeed, a
principal object of the sixteenth century became the pro-
motion of sheep farming. Arable land was laid down to
pasture, and grass holdings, instead of being held as heretofore in scattered strips, were consolidated and enlarged.
England was a nation of sheep farmers and weavers, and
parts of the country became distinguished by the now
familiar hedges, ditches and walls, instead of the open
fields so characteristic of feudal times.

Though in Tudor days only 516,000 acres were enclosed, the enclosure movement was one which brought about a major revolution in the character of rural life and the structure of its society. Under the new vogue of sheep farming, one shepherd with his dog was able to take the place of many ploughmen, with the result that when the landlord turned grazier, large numbers of wage-earning labourers lost their employment. This often caused real distress, and many of the frequent risings during the first half of the period were directly attributable to the enclosure movement. In consequence, Parliament made repeated and strenuous efforts to prevent both the conversion of arable land to pasture and the enclosures which invariably followed. But though the number of sheep to be owned by one man was strictly limited, it was easy to father the ownership of flocks on sons or servants, and a solitary furrow driven across new-laid pasture satisfied the law that it should be returned to tillage, and, though the legal deterrents were vigorously pursued, they failed entirely to check the enclosure movement. Moreover, the essence of the feudal system had been in its intimate connection between the Lord's estate and the community of unfree tenants who lived upon it. It was a rural organization based upon man's relation to the land, and regulated purely by the conditions of agricultural life. It was in no way designed for any progress, nor was progress either intended or possible. The primary purpose of the tenant was to provide labour for the cultivation of the home farm. But by 1500 the feudal owners had largely ceased to farm their great estates through dependant occupiers, and were in many cases letting their farms for money rents. The labourers themselves had long been commuting their labour services by money payments, and there was arising during this period a class of free tenantry hitherto unknown.

Partly as a result of the avarice of landlords, and partly as a result of violent fluctuations in the value of the gold and silver coinage, farm rents rose to an exorbitant level. For the farmer who could keep up with the times, convert his arable land to pasture, enclose it and graze it with sheep, these rack rents still left farming as a possibility, but there were many who, as a result, were forced to throw up their holdings. Obliged in consequence to beg from door to door, these small farmers went to swell the ranks of the thousands of displaced farm workers, and numbers of evicted smallholders, whose holdings had been lumped together to allow the formation of new and larger sheep farms. Many old manors were disintegrating, and the deserted village and decaying farmhouse became a common feature of the times. The enclosure of the commons had deprived the village farmer, whatever his class, of his only grazing, and the co-operative system of farming was breaking up, making the people no longer self-sufficient but dependent on what they could earn. So that for the bulk of the rural classes, country life before Elizabeth was not always that of 'Merrie England'. Shakespeare is rich in references to the vagabondage of the times. Nor were the great social evils arising from the Tudor enclosures mitigated by the dissolution of the monasteries. These alone had in any degree catered for the relief of the poor, and now that poverty was increasing, the monastic hospitality was gone.

When in 1558 Elizabeth came to the throne she found that, as a result of these changes, her country was suffering from a vast array of disorder. Throughout the southern counties were hosts of broken men finding constant ground for resentment in the enclosures and consequent evictions. Many were idle rogues who not only committed all manner of serious crime, but in many minor ways were proving a real nuisance in the country areas. Children were kidnapped, horses, pigs and hens were stolen, linen was taken from the line, men and women robbed by the wayside. These vagabonds were the ready supporters of every insurrection, and the problems that they created were a primary concern of many Tudor statesmen. In 1563, Elizabeth, with the *Statute of Apprentices,* and the wise and humane poor laws which followed it, helped the natural growth of wealth and industry throughout the country to put an end to this social danger and during her reign a great measure of peace and prosperity was restored to the countryside. The English wool trade had gained greatly in scope, and it was natural that farming should share in the concomitant general prosperity.

Moreover, though the change in the mode of cultivation brought about social embarrassment, it undoubtedly favoured production. One acre on enclosed land, farmed by a free tenant, produced as much as two under the old system of the open fields. A more careful and constant cultivation increased the number of hands required on the enclosed farm, and caused a recall of much of the surplus labour earlier flung off the land. Woollen manufacture was fast becoming an important element in the national wealth, and a system grew up under which the wealthy began to hire men to work for them, not in factories provided for the purpose, but in their own homes. Here they worked with their own tools and equipment upon materials provided for them by their employers, and thus there arose large classes of people who made their livings partly by spinning and weaving under the shelter of their own rooftops, and partly by the cultivation of a plot of land. Under Elizabeth more than four-fifths of the population lived in the rural parts of the country, but of these a fair proportion were engaged in this form of agricultural-industrial combination. Of the minority who lived in the towns many were engaged, at least for part of the time, in agricultural pursuits.

There is abundant evidence that as the reign advanced the landowning and landrenting portions of the community waxed prosperous and gained in power. Food in country houses was abundant, and the old universal diet of salt fish gave way to a greater consumption of meat, fresh fish and fowl. Every man of substance pulled down his old timber or wattle farmhouse and set up a new one of brick or stone. Country houses were nobly furnished and carpets began to supersede the filthy rushes of not so long before. The wooden trenchers of the earlier yeomanry were replaced by pewter or plate, and the pillow, previously greatly despised by the farmer, was now taken into general use. Even the old roof-hole, persistent since Saxon days, was replaced at last by the now-familiar chimney. But this prosperity of the rural classes was not universal. For many of the smaller gentry times were hard. Whilst prices were steeply rising, land revenues remained comparatively stable, with the result that land was frequently in the market. The buyers generally belonged to the rising middle classes of the towns, who, bringing with them into rural life a new spirit of enterprise, were destined to become the squirearchy and yeomanry of the seventeenth and eighteenth centuries.

Another class, that of the labourers, suffered, without compensation, from the rising prices of the time, and the dearness of agricultural produce. Their wages were fixed by the magistrates, according to the law, and the rates of pay followed but slowly the upward tendency of prices. Fortunately a change was taking place in their condition. Except in the north and east of the country where the old open-field system continued to be practised, farmers began to prefer to hire labourers by the day rather than board agricultural servants engaged for the year, as had been the custom. Hired thus at day rates, such labourers probably shared the general prosperity. Their hopes for the future lay in the increased demands for labour resulting from improved methods of agriculture. The whole period is one in which we have to hold in mind a somewhat imprecise picture of change going on beneath our eyes. Due to the lapse of the ancient labour services, the growth of trade and the division and change of ownership of manors mentioned, the latter were fast breaking up as economic and social units. Yet at the same time the law persisted in regarding the manor as remaining what it had always been—the fundamental unit of land organization. Through its system of courts, the manor continued long after the Tudors to preserve the rights of the peasantry as they had existed time out of mind.

WORKING MEN'S COLLEGE LIBRARY

VI

EDUCATION

T. L. JARMAN

ERHAPS the Tudor schoolboy was more fortunate than the boy of to-day. Perhaps the schoolroom reflected something of the splendour of the age: the discovering of lands beyond the sea, the excitements of new mental horizons, the genius of Elizabethan literature, the freshness of springtime in an England unspoiled as yet by factory and mine. And how much the Tudor schoolboy was spared—no modern studies overburdened the curriculum, no science, little mathematics, no modern languages, no geography, no history. Yet this fortunate creature, Shakespeare describes as

> . . . *the whining school-boy, with his satchel*
> *And shining morning face, creeping like snail*
> *Unwillingly to school.*

For if the Tudor boy escaped much which burdens the boy of to-day, he faced at school a curriculum at least as arduous and he studied in conditions much more rigorous. A few years before Shakespeare wrote, a boy at Winchester College described in Latin hexameters how he rose at

five, and after prayers at six, devoted himself to writing
Latin verses with his fellow pupils, each one of them
'chained as closely to his desk as Prometheus to the crag
on Caucasus'. Nor were there as yet any new-fangled
educational ideas to soften the physical terrors of learning. The 'best schoolmaster' was held to be 'the greatest
beater'.

To the historian the Tudors mark the beginning of
modern times. Leland, in his journeys through the
England of Henry VIII, observed the crumbling battle-
ments of feudal castles and the decaying walls of the
dissolved monasteries—'lofty towers downrazed'. But the
change from mediæval to modern was gradual. Universities, grammar schools, Public Schools, were all mediæval
in origin. In spite of the intellectual ferment of Renaissance and Reformation, the schools long remained
unchanged, in spirit, content and educational method.
Latin was the principal subject taught, and the grammar
school the most common educational institution.

In Tudor times education was still firmly based on
mediæval foundations, and of mediæval education the
dominant characteristic was its connection with the
Church. Education in the sense of book-learning—for
there are other senses—was in mediæval Christendom
something essentially ecclesiastical. Ancient Greece and
Rome had had their own, and very different, educational
ideal. They aimed at producing the balanced man,
trained in body and in mind. The Greeks thought of the
'good life' which was intellectual as well as physical and
spiritual. The gods had their place, but did not dominate
the living of man's life nor the ideal which determined
the training of his sons.

But from the collapse of the Roman Empire in the

fifth century until the Renaissance in the fifteenth, the
Roman Catholic Church established throughout Europe
a way of life in which the emphasis was placed not upon
the things of this world but upon those of the next.
Education was a powerful means of serving this new
ideal. To study the Bible the churchman must read the
Latin translation of St. Jerome. The Church needed
priests to perform its services, to perpetuate its worship,
to spread its teaching. The Barbarian conquerors who
broke up the Roman world were, for the most part,
uncouth and uneducated. The Roman Church had to
train the Barbarian conquerors for its service. Rome
bequeathed a language and a literature; the Church took
these and used them as instruments to achieve its own
religious end. In time, the illiterate conquerors found
they needed the help of literate men in the service of the
state. For this they were dependent on the Church, and
during many centuries the state was served in all save
war by churchmen. The schools and universities which
grew up during the Middle Ages were ecclesiastical
institutions: they were controlled and administered by
the Church, their teachers were churchmen in holy orders,
and most of those who were taught were destined to
become in their turn either priests or monks. The school
might be attached to a cathedral or taught by a parish
priest; it would teach Latin and perhaps some theology
and logic. In the universities, Latin and more advanced
studies in philosophy and theology were the subjects followed by the majority of students.

The religious and bookish character of education
lasted into Tudor times and was only gradually modified
during the sixteenth and later centuries. Essentially
bookish, it was the education of the priest, the clerk. It

WORKING MEN'S
COLLEGE
LIBRARY

Country Life

CAIUS COLLEGE, CAMBRIDGE
The Gate of Honour

THE SOUTH BANK OF THE THAMES

was the education of only one section of the mediæval population.

Mediæval society consisted of three classes or estates: nobles, clergy, commons. In writing of education we have so far thought only of the clergy; for them the Latin education was highly proper. For the nobles, however, there was quite another kind of education, and for the commons, at least for the peasants, there was none. The young noble might, or might not, learn to read and write his native tongue. Latin he would not know. Much more important for him was the training in chivalry: how to fight with lance and sword and shield, how to manage his heavy war-horse, and, as feudal life became rather more civilized, how to behave himself in court and how to deport himself with ladies. The lusty young squire or the vigorous feudal baron would have a certain contempt for that bookish man, the priest. The Church, too, was the only possible way of preferment for the poor man's son. There was thus a very clear determining factor of social class in the matter of education. The educational ideal was divided. 'In the ancient world culture and high birth went together. It was the grave misfortune of Europe in the Middle Ages that these two qualities admired of man were sharply dissociated. The business of the knight was to fight and hunt; the duty of the clerk was to pray and learn' (H. A. L. Fisher). Or, as the country squire of Tudor times bluntly expressed it: 'I would sooner see my son hanged than a bookworm. It is a gentleman's calling to be able to blow the horn, to hunt and hawk. He should leave learning to clodhoppers.' For weak and ailing sons, however, the universities might be a last resource.

This may account, to some extent, for the English-man's traditional dislike of education and contempt for schoolmasters. The schoolmaster is a bookish man, removed from the world of action and affairs; the pedant is a figure of fun. 'Who would be a schoolmaster that could live in any other way?' said a Cambridge graduate to Erasmus. And the bookish man was attacked from above and below. The noble regarded him as an inferior; the peasant disliked and feared what seemed to him a kind of lettered magic, which could be used to draw up contracts fixing villein service and tying the peasant to the soil. For this reason, lawyers, in particular, were disliked by the lower orders. Shakespeare illustrates the popular hatred of education in *King Henry VI,* when Smith the Weaver leads the Clerk of Chatham before the rebel leader, Jack Cade.

> *Smith.* The Clerk of Chatham: he can write and
> read, and cast accompt.
> *Cade.* O monstrous!
> *Smith.* We took him setting of boys' copies.
> *Cade.* Here's a villain!

But in spite of noble disdain and boorish derision, learning had established a place in mediæval society and universities and schools were accepted, and often honoured, institutions long before Tudor times. Oxford and Cambridge, the only English universities during and for long after the Tudor period, like their prototype the University of Paris, grew up during the twelfth century. Three Scottish universities date from the fifteenth: St. Andrews was founded in 1411, Glasgow in 1453, Aberdeen in 1494 (Edinburgh set up its university in Paris, but England has been more fortunate and the 1582). Nothing remains of the sixty mediæval colleges of collegiate foundations of Oxford and Cambridge are a splendid memorial of the Middle Ages. The sixteenth century was itself a great period for the creation of colleges. Wolsey, who as bursar of Magdalen had paid some of the bills for the famous tower and who was later master of Magdalen College School, himself founded Cardinal College, refounded by Henry VIII as Christchurch, perhaps the most imposing of Oxford colleges. At Cambridge, Henry VIII formed out of three existing foundations what was to become one of the most famous of colleges, Trinity. Christ's, St. John's and Magdalene, Cambridge, also date from this time; Emmanuel and Sidney Sussex came later with the rising tide of Protestantism after the Catholic reaction of Mary's reign. Brasenose and Corpus Christi, Oxford, date from 1509 and 1516 respectively; Jesus College at Oxford was set up by a Welshman in Elizabeth's day and with her support. At the end of Elizabeth's reign Sir Thomas Bodley founded his famous library in Oxford. The dissolution of the monasteries and chantries was at first a threat to the universities, which as religious houses were not altogether dissimilar in character. But the universities weathered the storm, and some monastic endowments were put towards the establishment of the new colleges.

In England, during the Renaissance many famous scholars graced the universities; sovereigns were themselves both patrons of learning and learned themselves. Henry VIII wrote in Latin a theological treatise against Luther; Edward VI was a studious boy; Elizabeth studied the classics industriously, and could make speeches both in Latin and Greek. The unhappy Lady Jane Grey was a learned and cultured woman. Erasmus, the most famous scholar and humanist of his day and a figure of universal repute, lectured at Cambridge on Greek. Among English scholars some were outstanding and are still commonly remembered, perhaps most of all Sir Thomas More, whose book *Utopia* has given its name to a whole class of political and social literature. But equally famous in their day were Dean Colet of St. Paul's, Grocyn, Fellow of New College and perhaps, as Erasmus hints, the first man to teach Greek at Oxford, and Linacre, eminent classical scholar and student of medicine. All these men and women were influenced by the 'new learning'; all were figures of the Renaissance.

The great movements of Renaissance and Reformation brought new subjects into the university curriculum. The revival of learning meant the introduction of the Greek language and literature, and something of the Greek spirit of free enquiry. With Greek came the idea of a liberal education. Latin had been studied for its vocational value, for it was the key to the learned professions. Greek, rather than offering any vocational improvement to its students, had its own cultural value and it now became a subject of humane studies, of *literae humaniores*. But Greek, as More pointed out in its defence, was also useful in New Testament study. For a time there was a struggle between old and new, between 'Trojans' and 'Greeks' in the universities. The conservatives supported the old curriculum of Latin, logic and theology, but gradually Greek established a place for itself. Hebrew, some physics and mathematics were also subjects of university study, and in the universities of Britain and northern Europe a new, Protestant theology took the place of the older Roman Catholic teaching.

The Statutes of Elizabethan Oxford and Cambridge give some idea of the subjects studied and what they included. The lecturer in Theology was to lecture on

'sound literature'. Greek was to include Homer, Isocrates, Demosthenes, Euripides and also grammar and
style. Hebrew covered the Hebrew Scriptures and
Hebrew grammar. Philosophy included Aristotle's
Politics and *Ethics* and something of ancient physical
science, and Civil Law, Rhetoric (based on Quintilian
and Cicero) and Dialectic are listed as subjects. Medicine
is to be based on Hippocrates or Galen. Mathematics
includes Arithmetic, Euclid, Astronomy and Cosmo-
graphy. It will be noted that all these subjects are based
on ancient writers; men looked for information almost
exclusively to the past.

Before the end of the Middle Ages England already
possessed a number of grammar schools and two foundations destined to be our most famous Public Schools.
G. M. Trevelyan estimates that in Chaucer's day there
were three or four hundred grammar schools in the
country, most of them very small. William of Wykeham,
Bishop of Winchester and Chancellor of England,
founded Winchester College in 1387. Henry VI founded
Eton in 1440. Winchester and Eton were not at first
markedly different from many humbler grammar schools;
the Latin curriculum, method and general character were
the same. But they were richer in material resources and
distinguished by their illustrious founders, and boys were
thus sent to these schools not only from their locality but
also from all parts of the country. Both schools regarded
their object as essentially religious: Winchester was
founded 'to the praise, glory and honour of the name of
the Crucified and of the most glorious Virgin Mary, His
Mother'; on Eton the King enjoined the duty of praying
'for our soul when we have migrated from this light . . .
and for the souls of all the faithful departed'. At Win-

chester we can observe from the start a number of the characteristics which are still claimed as distinguishing features of the Public Schools: the religious character of the school with services in its own chapel; the corporate life; the prefect system; and the close connection with the universities, for Wykeham also founded New College, Oxford, at which the scholars from Winchester were to complete their school study of Latin grammar by 'sacred theology, that in especial Christ may be preached more fervently and more frequently'.

The Tudor period was marked by the foundation, largely by private benefactors, of a number of grammar schools, some of which have since developed into well-known Public Schools. Among these are St. Paul's, founded about 1509 by Dean Colet, with William Lily, who wrote a Latin Grammar book which was widely used in schools for many years, as first High Master, and Christ's Hospital which, set up by Edward VI in the building of Grey Friar's Monastery, from a 'charity-school' soon became the famous 'blue-coat school'. Other schools afterwards famous were Shrewsbury founded in 1552, Bromsgrove refounded under Mary in 1556, Repton founded in 1559, Westminster 1560, Merchant Taylors' 1561, Rugby 1567, and Harrow 1571.

But in spite of these important foundations, it cannot be assumed that the Tudor period saw a great expansion in the total number of schools. The dissolution of collegiate churches and chantries (with the dissolution of the monasteries) actually destroyed or crippled a number of schools maintained by the priests attached to these establishments. Edward VI acquired a reputation as a founder of schools because his name was attached to some schools which survived or were refounded. Indeed

Trevelyan maintains that—'Another great chance had been missed. If all, or even half, the endowments of masses for the dead had been devoted to schools, and if at the same time those schools had been left with their old landed property, England would soon have had the best secondary education in the world, and the whole history of England and of the world might have been changed for the better.' It is an interesting speculation—one of the might-have-beens of history. But there is here, perhaps, a reading into the expression 'secondary education' of its modern and wider meaning. The secondary education of Tudor days was an education in Latin Grammar, which was a training for a narrow range of professions, the Church, law, and, to a limited extent, medicine. Mulcaster thought, in 1581, that there were already too many schools for the openings then available to scholars. It is permissible to doubt how far the multiplication of Latin grammar schools would have altered fundamentally the future of the world.

In the Tudor grammar school boys were taught to read, write and speak Latin; Latin was the most important subject of the curriculum. At the better schools, boys were required on admission to be able to read and write English. A certain amount of information about history and geography was acquired in studying the classical texts. Among the authors studied were Aesop (*The Fables*, in Latin), Cicero, Terence, Sallust, Virgil, Ovid; the *Colloquies* or *Dialogues* of Erasmus and Vives were read to train the pupil in a fluent Latin style. Lily's *Latin Grammar* was much used, and it is probable that Shakespeare studied it at school in Stratford.

Where Greek was studied, for example at Westminster, Xenophon, Isocrates, Demosthenes, Homer and Hesiod were read. Towards the end of Elizabeth's reign a Greek Grammar, compiled by Camden, the historian who was also headmaster of Westminster, came into use. It was adopted by Eton, and became known as the *Eton Greek Grammar*.

Naturally Tudor writers on education were supporters of classical education. Roger Ascham, public orator at Cambridge and tutor to Elizabeth, advocated translation and retranslation of Latin as the best method; Mulcaster, headmaster of Merchant Taylors' and later of St. Paul's, supported Latin but would also have given a place to English. John Brinsley, Puritan divine and schoolmaster at Ashby-de-la-Zouch, paid much attention to the parsing of Latin.

An intriguing question now arises: how far was provision made in Tudor England for elementary education? Boys admitted to grammar schools were often expected to be able already to read and write in English; this implies the existence of elementary schools or of elementary instruction elsewhere. But the position is obscure. There was, of course, no general system of education until the nineteenth century. However, in mediæval times England developed an important wool trade with Europe; in Italy and northern Europe there were cities with banking and merchant houses whose ships traded to the Levant or the Baltic. Merchants, bankers, craftsmen, clerks must have had a degree of elementary education. Where did they get it?

In Florence, already in the fourteenth century, Villani tells of schools teaching reading and calculation; in the fifteenth century, Hamburg, Lübeck and Brunswick possessed schools to teach reading and writing in German. Two schools to include in their curriculum writing and reckoning are heard of in fifteenth-century Yorkshire. Probably, too, Song Schools for choirboys and also chantry priests gave elementary instruction, and some teaching may have been given at home. By Tudor times the horn-book was in use—an alphabet framed in wood and covered with a plate of transparent horn.

It is fairly certain that a knowledge of English reading was fairly widespread in the sixteenth century. The *Paston Letters,* a correspondence in which a number of people took part between 1422 and 1509, are letters of people who could write in English. And in 1477 Caxton set up his printing press and turned out many books 'in our English language'. He had readers in English, and where there were readers there must have been education.

The effects of the Renaissance and Reformation on schools were not as great as might be supposed. Many features of mediæval education persisted into Tudor times. Latin remained the dominant subject in the grammar schools, though Greek began to find its way in. Greek was taught, for example, at St. Paul's, Westminster and Harrow. The Roman writer on education, Quintilian, became an influence and strengthened the hold of the classics, for Quintilian stressed the value of oratory; the orator (statesman, politician, lawyer) must be learned but must also be able to express his knowledge in speech. The Reformation which split the old religious unity led to a struggle, on the Continent, for control of education. Luther and Melanchthon wrote on education, but, in that they looked to the past and accepted its basic Latin teaching, they were not pioneers. In the Roman Catholic world, for three centuries to come, the Jesuit Order used the schools it maintained in its struggle against Protestantism; the Jesuit schools were considered the best in Europe, but their curriculum was still based on Latin and theology.

As yet, and for long after Tudor times, there was little change in the grammar schools. Natural Science, for example, was quite ignored. At the end of Elizabeth's reign William Gilbert, a supporter of the new Copernician theory, was writing on magnetism, and Bacon published his *Advancement of Learning,* in which he advocated the experimental method as the means of discovering scientific truths. But this did not affect the school curriculum. There was, however, a considerable amount of theorizing about the growing need for a new kind of education. The great Spanish scholar, Vives, for a time in England as tutor to Mary when princess, studied and wrote on psychology. From Italy came Castiglione's book *Il Cortegiano* (the courtier) and with it the Doctrine of Courtesy. Similar books appeared elsewhere, notably *The Boke named the Governour* by Sir Thomas Elyot. By the courtier was meant the man of affairs, who served his prince. For such a man the old book learning of the grammar school was not enough. He needed also to be trained in the exercises of war; mathematics and science were becoming necessary to the soldier; and for the diplomat modern languages, law, history and geography were all of increasing importance. A new kind of school— the Academy—is suggested. Academies sprang up in France and Germany during the seventeenth century. In England, much earlier, Sir Humphrey Gilbert had urged a project for a 'Queen Elizabeth's Academy', but it came to nothing. As Professor Adamson says, 'England was among the very last to admit modern studies to the schools which educated her governing class'. Throughout the Tudor period, and for long afterwards, the grammar school and Latin grammar were dominant in British education.

WORKING MEN'S COLLEGE LIBRARY

VII

SCIENCE

JEAN LINDSAY

To limit a study of science to Tudor times is to cramp into a political and dynastic frame a subject which has quite other limits of its own. To treat of sixteenth-century science in England alone is to focus attention on a quiet backwater when events of great importance were taking place in the main stream. If science in Tudor England is to have any serious meaning it must signify what science Englishmen of that period were taught, what revolutionary scientific ideas they might be expected to discuss during their lifetime and what scientific conceptions coloured their ordinary speaking and writing rather than what original contributions they themselves made.

In the sixteenth century scientific thought was in a cauldron. As far back as in the fourteenth century criticism had begun against the generally accepted Aristotelian system, and in the sixteenth century criticisms and new hypotheses came in a rush. Accepted views were overturned, but it was not until the end of the seventeenth century, when Newton completed the work that Galileo had done much to set forward, that a coherent new system was generally accepted. The sixteenth century was a period of a profusion of conflicting new opinions, and great uncertainty, for old opinions died hard, and so far as the current ideas of the poets and dramatists were concerned it was the old ideas of Aristotle or Bartholomew the Englishman that coloured men's speech.

Of these old ideas five were the most outstanding. In astronomy men conceived of a finite universe with the earth at its centre. It was also very generally believed that the heavenly bodies had an occult influence over the destinies of men and nations which could only be rightly interpreted by the astrologer. In dynamics, they believed that local movement was only possible if a mover existed and so were led to postulate the existence of 'Intelligences' each moving one of the planets. In physics they supposed every physical object to be made up of a combination of two or more of the four elements, earth, air, fire and water, and this found an echo in the medical belief that man's health depended on a proper balance between the four humours cold, hot, moist and dry. In Chemistry, men's views were almost totally clouded by a belief in the claims of the alchemist who was supposed to be able to find the Philosopher's Stone and the Elixir of Life. Even in departments where men had plenty of practical experience, as in those of medicine, zoology and botany, the sixteenth century was still clogged with a mass of superstitious moralizing fables about all animals from the cat to the salamander and a belief that plants had all been created in order to cure some special disease and that the plant's purpose could be found by studying it carefully, for every plant bore in its structure a 'signature' showing what it was meant to cure.

In one aspect of science geography-development took place during the sixteenth century because the mass of new material which became available did not conflict with any of the accepted philosophical or religious ideas. The voyages of Dias round Cape Horn in 1486, of Columbus who landed somewhere in the West Indies in 1492, of Da Gama who reached India in 1497, to say nothing of the Englishmen who reached Newfoundland in 1497, or Muscovy in 1533 were the most outstanding of a mass of explorations which expanded man's experience by literally including within it a new world. Columbus had relied on mediæval geographical writings which his experience and the explorations of a generation of Spaniards such as Cortez and Pizarro and Magellan showed to have seriously underestimated the distance between Europe and the eastern coast of Asia. The desire to make good these errors combined with the intellectual stimulus resulting from the rediscovery of Ptolemy's geographical writings at the end of the fifteenth century to encourage men to produce a series of very fine new maps of the world. Shakespeare made use of one of these in which many rhumb lines were marked when in *Twelfth Night* he wanted to ridicule Malvolio's foolish smiling: 'he doth smile his face into more lines than are in the new map with the augmentation of the Indies'. The geographers found a new device for projecting a spherical globe on a two dimensional sheet. In 1569 Mercator hit on a device which would compensate for the distortions imposed on him and would thus produce a map on which the course of a ship would cut the meridians at the same angle as on a sphere. Cartography also benefited from the developments in practical surveying which took place at this time. As early as the fourteenth century the cross staff and compass had been used for surveying, and in the sixteenth century a German cartographer produced maps of Lorraine and the Rhineland which were so accurate that they seem likely to have been produced by some method of surveying by the use of instruments. The Cosmographer to the Emperor claimed in 1533 that he had devised a method of surveying which needed no direct measurement, and when Saxton (*fl.* 1570–1596) made his survey for the maps of the counties of England in the 1570's he was given special facilities for going up church towers and other points of vantage to survey by means of triangulations.

Developments in astronomy and cosmology were accompanied by more controversy. The position of the heavenly bodies was a matter of immediate concern to many people in Tudor times and even if they did not all take astrology as seriously as did the Emperor Rudolf or the Earl of Leicester its ideas shot through their common speech. People thought of themselves as born under a particular star, though they did not all put it with such charm as Beatrice in *Much Ado About Nothing* when she said, 'There was a star danced, and under that I was born'. Lear's sad dictum that 'the stars above us govern our condition' would have been very generally accepted as true as would have been Calpurnia's assertion that 'the heavens themselves blaze forth the death of princes'. Certainly there were other men strong-minded as Cassius when he affirmed that 'the fault dear Brutus is not in our stars but in ourselves that we are underlings' or who nodded cynical agreement when Lear repudiated a belief in astrological influences as cowardice and 'an admirable evasion of the whore master man to lay his goatish disposition to the charge of a star', but generally opinion supported the belief in the influences of the planets, and was disturbed at the astronomical theories which in the sixteenth century upset the whole basis of astrology as well as coming into conflict with more reputable religious beliefs by calling into question whether the earth were in fact at the centre of the universe.

During the centuries which had elapsed since the geo-centric theories of the structure of the universe had been put forward by such ancient philosophers as Plato, Aris-totle and Ptolemy observers had brought forward many facts which did not fit into any of their systems. The differ-ences in brightness of the various planets, the fact that a solar eclipse is sometimes total and sometimes annular both conflicted with the idea that the earth was at the centre of a universe in which the planets revolved always at the same distance from the centre. The procession of the equinoxes presented another problem. In order to fit the theory to the observed phenomena, to 'save the phenomena', various astronomers had tried to work out modifications until the number of circles necessary was 56. Some thinkers suggested that although the earth was the centre of the universe the planets need not revolve about it as their centre, but that this centre might be fixed on a line drawn from the centre of the earth to the sun. This was known as the theory of the movable eccentric. An alternative theory was that the planet moved in a circle whose centre moved in another circle and so on until a last circle was reached which was at rest in relation to the earth but whose centre need not coincide with the centre of the earth. The path of the planet was the epicycle, and the last circle the deferent. It is to these complications that Milton referred in *Paradise Lost* when Adam and the Archangel Raphael had their long dis-

WORKING MEN'S
COLLEGE
LIBRARY

HENRY VIII CONFERRING A CHARTER UPON THE SURGEONS COMPANY

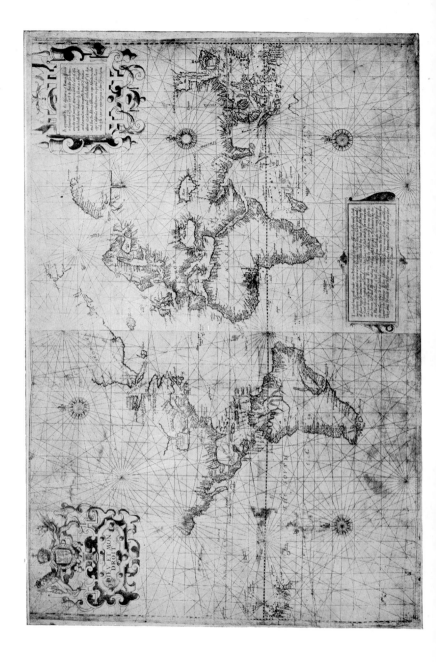

cussion on the nature of the universe. The Archangel rebuked Adam for scribbling the design of the universe with centric and eccentric, cycle and epicycle, and the debate was left undecided as to whether the earth or the sun was really at the centre of the system. Marlowe makes Dr. Faustus put Mephistopheles through a series of questions on the same theme, and in the course of this discussion occurs the description:

> 'the spheres
> *Mutually folded in each other's orb . . .*
> *All jointly move upon one axel tree*
> *Whose termine is termed the world's wide pole'.*

The complexity of the system provoked scholars to try to find some simpler solution of the observable facts. Those who were influenced by the Platonic ideas which were returning to fashion in Italy in the late fifteenth century were specially eager to find a simpler explanation, for they believed that the universe could be explained as a mystical harmony of numbers or of geometrical arrangements of units of space. Copernicus (1473–1543) had studied in Italy and produced a theory which explained the observable facts by supposing that the centre of the whole system was the sun rather than the earth. There seems to have been some mystical symbolism which encouraged Copernicus to put the sun at the most honourable place in the cosmic system, but by reducing the earth to a position of very secondary importance he undermined the beliefs of the astrologers and threw doubts on the teachings of the Church. But at first his theory did not arouse much comment. It was welcomed as early as 1556 by some English scholars such as Robert Recorde (*c.* 1510–1558), John Field (*c.* 1525–

1587) and John Dee (1527–1608), and another Englishman, Thomas Digges (d. 1595), repeated this support of it
in 1571 when he ridiculed the Ptolemaic or geocentric
system by comparing it to 'a set of hands, head and feet
taken off different men'; but as late as 1605 Francis Bacon
(1561–1626) could seriously reject Copernicus' hypothesis
in favour of a geocentric system of his own.

A theory much more subversive of established religious
beliefs was put forward by Giordano Bruno (1547–1600)
in three little pamphlets published in England in 1584.
He accepted the hypothesis that the planets moved round
the sun as the centre, but denied that it therefore followed
that the sun was the centre of the whole universe. Bruno
argued that the universe was infinite and that it therefore
could have no centre. For him the sun was moving like
all the other planets and there might easily be other
worlds and solar systems with their centres in some of the
fixed stars. To a generation accustomed to think of the
universe as finite and as having been created by a God
who must necessarily be apart from his creation Bruno's
ideas that the universe was impregnated with a soul in all
its parts, and that it was infinite and therefore could not
have been created were shocking in the extreme. Pascal's
cry, 'Le silence éternal de ces espaces infinis m'effraye',
takes on a new poignancy when read in this context.

'The seventeenth century opened lurid with the flames
that made Giordano's shroud', but his fate was not to
discourage other astronomers from speculating on the
structure of the universe and already before the end of
the sixteenth century two men had achieved notable
advances on the hypotheses put forward by Copernicus.
Tycho Brahe (1546–1601) carried out a series of more
accurate observations than had been made up till that

time on the movements of the heavenly bodies, and put forward a very complicated hypothesis of his own to account for them. Kepler (1571–1630) perfected the mathematical processes necessary to resolve the problems of cosmology but was only able to put forward an unsatisfactory compromise between the various conflicting hypotheses himself. English scholars such as Digges, Thomas Harriot (1560–1621) and Sir Henry Wotton (1568–1639) kept in touch with what was going on in Denmark and the Empire, and may indeed have used something like a telescope a decade before it was made by the Dutchman Lippershey in 1608 or by Galileo in 1609, but they were not able to supply the new synthesis for which the European astronomers were waiting. That was to be the work of another Englishman, but Newton had not been born by the end of the sixteenth century.

If it took a long time before the mediæval astronomical hypotheses were overthrown in favour of the Copernican and Newtonian, it took an equally long time before the mediæval ideas of dynamics were altered. The debate began in fourteenth-century Paris with such men as Jean Buridan, but it was not ended even by Galileo and went on well into the seventeenth century till the new hypothesis were clearly stated by Descartes. In this field as in astronomy the Tudor Period was one of conflicting interpretations. In physics enough progress had been made for a clash to be possible, and very little was done to modify the mediæval ideas of the nature of matter until Boyle published his *Sceptical Chemist* in 1661. During most of the Middle Ages medicine had been closely linked with studies in astrology: The universities of Padua and Montpellier had been famous as centres for both studies. In the sixteenth century physicians were coming to be

able to diagnose an increasing number of diseases; Caius
(1510–1573) wrote a very clear pamphlet on the sweating
sickness. Fracastoro (1483–1553) had enunciated a theory
of germ infection.

In medicine as in botany and zoology the Tudor period
was still living in the shadow of the Middle Ages, and
though some progress was made in accuracy of description
and classification, Shakespeare's natural history was that
of Bartholomew the Englishman and his medicine
enshrined the Aristotelian idea of humours. Thersites
in one of his fits of cursing speaks among others of the
rotton diseases of the south, guts griping, ruptures,
catarrhs, raw eyes, dirt rotten livers and wheezing lungs.
Elsewhere Shakespeare mentions palsy, both as meaning
paralysis agitans and the result of a stroke, consumption
when he notes the strange sweet smell of the breath of a
tubercular patient, and compares it with the smell of the
atmosphere of the enchanted island in *The Tempest*;
he also mentions gout, ague, the sweating sickness, and
the red pestilence with its death tokens by which it is
thought he meant bubonic plague.

As early as 1518 the College of Physicians had been
founded in London and in Tudor England many distinguished physicians were in practice. Some of these,
like Linacre (*c.* 1460–1524) or Harvey (1578–1657), had
graduated at Padua, others at Montpellier, Leyden, Basle
or Heidelberg. But still the treatment of disease was a
very uncertain business and little progress in internal
medicine had been made during the Middle Ages. Para-
celsus (1493–1641), who adopted his Latin name to show
that he meant to eclipse the great Celsus (*fl.c.* A.D. 30) and
whose own Swiss name of Bombastus has given an adjec-
tive to the language, claimed to have done a great deal to

inaugurate a new system of treatment, and publicly burnt the works of Galen before beginning a course of lectures, and did in fact do much to encourage the use of mineral drugs and especially antimony; but his works were so obscure and so confused with alchemy that he had less influence than might have been expected from the force of his character.

It was in anatomy rather than in the treatment of disease that the sixteenth century showed a spectacular advance. The Netherlander Andreas Wesel or Vesalius (1514–1564), having studied at Paris, where he received a thorough training in Galenic anatomy, went to Padua where he became a professor and there in a few short years did the work and wrote the book which began a new period in anatomical studies. Vesalius was a very skilful dissector and put his own hand to the work instead of leaving it to be done by a demonstrator while the professor read his lecture. He was also fortunate to have secured the help of an artist who drew most beautiful plates which enormously increased the value of his book. This also showed Vesalius' independence of mind since he insisted on having his book illustrated at a time when this was officially frowned on by many high medical authorities.

The inspiration of beautiful drawings also did much to encourage the study of botany, though here the advance was nothing like as spectacular as that achieved in anatomy. Botanical studies in England had declined during the Middle Ages from Anglo-Saxon times when the Anglo-Saxon leechdoms had contained the names of far more flowers than any contemporary Latin or German works, but in the sixteenth century there was a revival. In 1548 William Turner, the father of English Botany

(d. 1568), published his Names of Herbs in which he made the first attempt to give accurate descriptions of familiar flowers and to fix their names. In 1554 Dodoens (1518–1585) produced a Dutch herbal and in 1578 a translation of this was produced by Henry Lyte (c. 1529–1607). In 1571 Lobel (1538–1616), a countryman of Dodoens, produced a herbal intended not for country gentlemen with an interest for medicine but for serious students. In 1577 appeared Frampton's *Joyful News out of the New Found World,* containing particulars of many strange plants. In 1597 came the famous herbal of Gerard (1545–1612). As yet there was no attempt to classify plants according to their natural characteristics, though Bacon hinted at the possibility in *Sylva Sylvarum,* and there were still some very strange opinions, such as the one that the mandrake when it was pulled from the ground gave a shriek which was fatal to anyone who heard it. To get the mandragona mentioned by Cleopatra men tied the top of the plant to the collar of a dog which pulled to get away and dragged up the mandrake. But though such mediæval beliefs still persisted among some people with the publication of beautifully and accurately illustrated herbals botanical studies moved out of the moralizing period into that of collecting.

Zoology was moving in the same direction under the inspiration of the great Swiss Gesner (1516–1565), though Dr. Caius could still write to him reporting on a strange beast that had been brought to England by some Norwegian sailors that, though they claimed that it was an elk, this could not be the case, for as everyone knew Caesar had said that the elk had no joints in its legs and this animal certainly had. The speech of the time showed that many other strange legends were still familiar enough to serve as similies: the bear cub carried no impression of its dam until she had licked it into shape, the unicorn could be betrayed by trees and bears with glasses, though scholars have suggested that Shakespeare meant tigers and had got the legends confused. Swans died, and on the edge of the regular established zoological world were a host of mythical creatures, leviathans, basilisks, phoenixes, cockatrices and dragons. Even the animal world was invaded with the physical ideas which were beginning to become old-fashioned. The colour of a horse depended on the proportion of the humours within it. 'If earth predominates he is melancholy, heavy and faint-hearted and his colour is black, russet, a bright or dark dun. If he has more of water he is phlegmatic, slow, dull, apt to lose flesh and his colour is usually white. If of the air, he is sanguine, pleasant, nimble and of a bay colour. If of the fire, he is choleric, therefore light, hot and fiery, a stirer seldom of great strength and a bright sorrel colour.' The best horses were those in which the elements were equally mixed, when the colour was brown bay, dapple grey, black full of silver hairs or roan.

In sum the Tudor period of science was one in which old ideas persisted though some of them had long been criticized. It saw the achievements of Copernicus, Tycho Brahe, Vesalius, Columbus, even some of the work of Galileo himself, but with these ideas, not as yet, worked into a new synthesis capable of superseding that of Aristotle. The outlook of Tudor gentlemen had still more in common with the man of the Middle Ages than with that of the modern man of science.

WORKING MEN'S COLLEGE LIBRARY

VIII

POETRY

DOUGLAS GRANT

THE sun's diffused light can be reduced by a burning-glass to one spot, but the particle of fire and the glimmer of brilliance which the glass collects can only hint at the majestic properties of the original. English poetry blazed from its meridian during the reign of Queen Elizabeth, and an essayist who attempts to transcribe its splendour must be contented if he captures a particle and a glimmer.

The dawn of this great poetry at the beginning of the sixteenth century was overcast and uncertain. The poets, such as they were, had lost their art, and the heavy verses which they made, and which they were praised for making, can give us little delight. The exception was John Skelton (c. 1460–1529), the poet laureate, a man of distinct personality, who wrote with wit and consummate delicacy. His finest poems are those in which he used a nimble doggerel—'sportive' verse 'run wild'—which disguises but cannot hide his skill. The freshness and spontaneity of his inspiration, the unaffected simplicity of his sentiment, and the good-humoured mockery which he shows in his lighter satirical pieces, are essentially English. His wit is to be seen in his poem *The Sparrow's Dirge*, which, while humorously bewailing the death of a bird, hints at greater sorrows; his delicacy in the verses which he delighted to address to children, a subject peculiarly fitted to his genius, and in his lines to *Mistress Margaret Hussey*, he has caught the jubilant, pure spirit of maidenhood:

> *Merry Margaret, as midsummer flower,*
> *Gentle as falcon or hawk of the tower,*
> *With solace and gladness,*
> *Much mirth and no madness,*
> *All good and no badness;*
> *So joyously,*
> *So maidenly,*
> *So womanly,*
> *Her demeaning;*
> *In every thing*
> *Far far passing*
> *That I can indite*
> *Or suffice to write*
> *Of merry Margaret, as midsummer flower,*
> *Gentle as falcon or hawk of the tower.*

There were, meanwhile, assembling at the Court of Henry VIII a number of young, noble poets who were to introduce a profound change into English poetry. A later lyricist, Thomas Campion (1567–1620), might be thought to refer to them, and to the direction which poetry took under their guidance, when he exclaimed:

> *But stay! now I discern they go on a pilgrimage*
> *Towards Love's holy land, fair Paphos or Cyprus.*

Such devotion is meet for a blithesome age;
With sweet youth it agrees well to be amorous.
Let old angry fathers lurk in an hermitage.
Come, we'll associate this jolly pilgrimage.

These new poets made their pilgrimage to 'Love's holy land' through Italy. The Renaissance—that triumphant resurgence of the human spirit—had earlier freed the Italian poets from mediæval encumbrances, and the subtle melodies and introspective sensuality of their verse fascinated the English poets, who felt that they still 'lurked in an hermitage'. The first poets to imitate successfully the Italians were Sir Thomas Wyatt (*c.* 1503-1542), and Henry Howard, Earl of Surrey (1517?-1547). These two—in the words of an Elizabethan critic—'having . . . tasted the sweete and stately measures and stile of the Italian poesie . . . greatly pollished our rude and homely manner of vulgar poesie from what it had been before'. Wyatt and Surrey attempted to refine and burnish their diction until, rid of its native roughnesses and clumsy redundancies, it could express sweetly those amatory ideas which they wished to copy from the Italian poets.

Wyatt is, without question, the finer poet of the two. His command of lyric measures, his subtlety of thought and sensation, and his expressive skill are remarkable; and the courtly grace of his own personality lends to his works an unique savour. A short example of his quality is the poem *His Reward*:

With serving still
This have I won
For my goodwill
To be undone.

And for redress
   Of all my pain,
Disdainfulness
   I have again.

And for reward
   Of all my smart,
Lo, thus unheard
   I must depart!

Wherefore all ye
   That after shall
By fortune be
   As I am thrall,

Example take
   What I have won;
Thus for her sake
   To be undone.

Surrey has neither the innate grace nor the sharp sentiment which distinguishes Wyatt, but he made, nevertheless, an original contribution to the development of English poetry. He handled the sonnet with greater mastery than Wyatt; he introduced through his translation of the *Aeneid* the use of blank verse, which was to become the supreme instrument of the great dramatists; and he had a fine appreciation for nature, which he showed in these lines taken from his sonnet on *Spring*:

The soote season, that bud and bloom forth brings,
   With green hath clad the hill and eke the vale.
The nightingale with feathers new she sings;
   The turtle to her mate hath told her tale.
Summer is come, for every spray now springs.
   The hart hath hung his old head on the pale;

The buck in brake his winter coat he flings;
  The fishes float with new repaired scale. . . .

These two poets started the pilgrimage, but no sooner had it begun than its progress was retarded by political confusion. The Reformation, with its display of wasteful greed, the contention for supremacy under the impotent reign of Edward VI, and the religious uncertainty and persecution which Queen Mary's policy involved, contributed to distract attention from poetry to mundane perplexities. Instability, too, infected the early years of Queen Elizabeth's reign, but as she won her people's affection, restored to them their independence, and, with unparalleled political wisdom, furthered their greatness, confidence returned; and suddenly, like the sun striking through routed clouds, the whole poetical firmament was ablaze.

The Queen herself inspired poetry. Her romantic virginity, her matchless character, the pageantry in which she surrounded her life, and her own delight in music and verse, roused every poet to sing her praises, and each, imagining himself to be a suitor for her favours, vied with the rest to express his adoration. She was commemorated under an hundred names, and worshipped with a fervour as great as that paid on the Continent to the Virgin Mary. Directly or indirectly, she was poetry's theme, and Edmund Spenser (1552?–1599) did not flatter when he made her the fourth Grace:

> *Lo, how finely the Graces can it foot*
>   *To the instrument;*
> *They dancen deftly, and singen soote,*
>   *In their merriment.*
> *Wants not a fourth Grace, to make the dance even?*

Let that room to my Lady be yeven:
  She shall be a Grace,
  To fill the fourth place,
And reign with the rest in heaven.

There quickly gathered about her poets who continued and enriched the courtly tradition begun by Wyatt and Surrey. They each had their ideal mistress, some virgin handmaid to the Queen, who cruelly rebuffed, while courteously encouraging, their hope; and, in verses remarkable for their range and intensity, they wept or praised, complained or rejoiced, according to the progress of their illimitable love. Their acknowledged leader—the type of all Elizabethan poetry and chivalry—was Sir Philip Sidney (1554–1586), whose graceful person, consummate manners, taste, and intelligence, made him 'the world's delight'. He addressed to his mistress, whom he called *Stella*, while taking to himself the name of *Astrophel*, a series of songs and sonnets which were the example to all amatory poets. His sonnets, in which he excelled, are rich in imagery, subtle in their perception of love's effects, and liquid in sound. This is among the best:

Highway, since you my chief Parnassus be,
  And that my Muse, to some ears not unsweet,
Tempers her words to trampling horses' feet
  More oft than to a chamber-melody,
Now, blessed you, bear onward blessed me
  To her, where I my heart, safe left, shall meet;
  My Muse and I must you of duty greet
With thanks and wishes, wishing thankfully.
Be you still fair, honoured by public heed;
  By no encroachment wronged, nor time forgot;

Nor blamed for blood, nor shamed for sinful deed;
And, that you know I envy you no lot
Of highest wish, I wish you so much bliss,
Hundreds of years you Stella's feet may kiss!

He showed the same versatility in his songs, and, since he
was curious to introduce into English poetry as many
stanza forms as the classical poets and Italians had successfully practised, he greatly increased its scope.

Although no other courtly poet surpassed Sidney's
achievements, some, and particularly his friend Fulke
Greville, Lord Brooke (1554–1628), wrote admirably.
Lord Brooke's verse has neither the delicacy nor the
melody of Sidney's, but it is distinguished by its deeper
thought—so deep that at times the movement of the poem
is slowed up by its impediment—and his best work is
notable for its intellectual acuity and richness of texture.

Charles Lamb's description of Sidney's amatory verses
could be applied equally to all Elizabethan poetry: his
poems, Lamb wrote, 'are stuck full of amorous fancies . . .
for True Love thinks no labour to send out Thoughts
upon the vast and more than Indian voyages, to bring
home rich pearls, outlandish wealth, gums, jewels,
spicery'. The Elizabethan seamen, heroic and outrageous,
returned with real 'outlandish wealth' from their 'Indian
voyages', and the effect of this wealth and these voyages
upon the poetic imagination of their contemporaries is
incalculable. Europe, an hundred years earlier, had been
barricaded within impassable seas, but the seamen had
since then pierced beyond into the remotest lands, and
the tales of the foreign splendour which they had seen—
and the wealth with which they returned witnessed in
part to their veracity—quickened the imagination into

fantastic life. The Elizabethans were alert to contest the supremacy of these new-found lands, and as they succeeded in engrossing more treasure, the poets, as though they had determined to catalogue this wealth, increased the variety of their imagery. A keen delight in every sensual richness invaded their work, and they ransacked the merchandise which they saw unloaded, or heard described, to satisfy this lust. Christopher Marlowe (1564–1593), whose violent and licentious character is typical of the Elizabethan adventurers, when he described Hero's accoutrement, in his noble translation of *Hero and Leander,* might have been drawing up an inventory of her bizarre wardrobe:

> *The outside of her garments were of lawn,*
> *The lining purple silk, with gilt stars drawn;*
> *Her wide sleeves green, and bordered with a grove*
> *Where Venus in her naked glory strove . . .*
> *Upon her head she ware a myrtle wreath,*
> *From whence her veil reached to the ground*
> *   beneath.*
> *Her veil was artificial flowers and leaves,*
> *Whose workmanship both man and beast*
> *   deceives . . .*
> *About her neck hung chains of pebble-stone,*
> *Which, lightened by her neck, like diamonds*
> *   shone . . .*
> *Buskins of shells all silvered used she,*
> *And branched with blushing coral to the knee,*
> *Where sparrows perched, of hollow pearl and gold,*
> *Such as the world would wonder to behold.*

The Elizabethan voyages, however, did not divert entirely the poets' attention to what was outlandish; they

contributed by their success to a great surge of patriotic
sentiment, which impelled the poets to celebrate the
natural loveliness and heroic history of their island.
Edmund Spenser, in his magnificent poem *The Faerie
Queene,* chose for his heroes and heroines those fabulous
characters associated with Prince Arthur and his Court,
and into their company he introduced Queen Elizabeth
and her courtiers. The poem is a paean in praise of
England's past and present glory, and if the adroit flattery
of the Queen is too obvious, it was deserved. *The Faerie
Queen* is no longer read for the leisurely evolution of the
story's glittering complications, but for its supreme verbal
harmonies, for the pageantry of the separate scenes, and
for its felicitous descriptions of the countryside through
which the characters proceed. Throughout its six long
books with their countless incidents, Spenser rhymes so
matchlessly, demonstrates such copious language, and
reveals such pure sentiments, that a reader must be content to praise him with ejaculations of wonder, or by
referring to his poetry his own description of music:

> *The whiles a most delicious harmony*
> *In full strange notes was sweetly heard to sound,*
> *That the rare sweetness of the melody*
> *The feeble senses wholly did confound,*
> *And the frail soul in deep delight nigh drowned.*

The entire treasury of Elizabethan imagery and vocabulary was dispersed about his poem, and he used it with
the freedom of a man born a great heir. This is his
description of Prince Arthur's helmet:

> *His haughty helmet, horrid all with gold,*
> *Both glorious brightness and great terror bred;*

WORKING MEN'S
COLLEGE
LIBRARY

GEORGE GASCOIGNE PRESENTING HIS
HEMETES THE HEREMYTE TO QUEEN ELIZABETH
About 1579

SIR PHILIP SIDNEY
1577(?) By an unknown artist

For all the crest a dragon did enfold
*   With greedy paws, and over all did spread*
*   His golden wings; his dreadful hideous head,*
Close couched on the beaver, seemed to throw
*   From flaming mouth bright sparkles fiery red,*
That sudden horror to faint hearts did show;
And scaly tail was stretched adown his back full
*   low.*

His rural freshness and simplicity are to be found in this stanza, whose very sound is that of clear, running water:

The joyous birds, shrouded in cheerful shade,
*   Their notes unto the voice attempered sweet;*
Th' angelical soft trembling voices made
*   To th' instruments divine, respondence meet;*
*   The silver sounding instruments did meet*
With the bass murmur of the waters' fall;
*   The waters' fall with difference discreet,*
Now soft, now loud, unto the wind did call;
The gentle warbling wind low answered to all.

The pride in their country which inspired the poets was closely linked to a delight in its language. The English tongue at this time seemed to break spontaneously into song, and the poets had no sooner thought than, with 'respondence meet', the words came to add melody to their ideas. Every man was potentially a poet, and the number of verses which have the signature *anonymous* show how many must have realized, if only in one perfect lyric, their innate powers. The graceful fluency of these song-writers ran on without pause, and, bewildered with such diversity and excellence, it is only possible to point out the main themes with which they

were preoccupied. They sang, like Anthony Munday
(*c.* 1553–1633), their mistress's unsurpassable beauty:

> *I serve a mistress whiter than the snow,*
>   *Straighter than cedar, brighter than the glass,*
> *Finer in trip and swifter than the roe,*
>   *More pleasant than the field of flowering grass;*
> *More gladsome to my withering joys that fade,*
> *Than winter's sun or summer's cooling shade.*

This sensuous and joyous indulgence in the present was,
however, always tempered by the imminent threat of
death, and, like Thomas Lodge (*c.* 1557–1625), they were
quick to warn their audience how little time there was to
enjoy this life:

> *Pluck the fruit and taste the pleasure,*
>   *Youthful lordings, of delight;*
> *Whilst occasion gives you seizure,*
>   *Feed your fancies and your sight:*
>   *After death, when you are gone,*
>   *Joy and pleasure is there none.*

They did not always address 'lordings', but they had songs
as well, like those of John Lyly (*c.* 1554–1606), for

> *Cross gartered swains, and dairy girls,*
> *With faces smug, and round as pearls.*

What they sang was, however, always expressed with the
same unpremeditated art that had its source in the sheer
pleasure which inspired George Peele (*c.* 1557–1596) to
write:

> *When as the rye reach to the chin,*
>   *And chopcherry, chopcherry ripe within,*
> *Strawberries swimming in the cream,*

And school-boys playing in the stream;
Then O, then O, then O my true love said,
Till that time come again,
She could not live a maid.

All these songs were written for music, and it is not surprising that the great Elizabethan lyricist was also a musician. Thomas Campion (1567–1620) matched sound and sense so flawlessly that his verse has the timeless, evocative quality of true perfection:

When to her lute Corinna sings,
Her voice revives the leaden strings,
And doth in highest notes appear,
As any challenged echo clear.
But when she doth of mourning speak,
E'en with her sighs the strings do break.

And as her lute doth live or die,
Led by her passion, so must I.
For when of pleasure she doth sing,
My thoughts enjoy a sudden spring;
But if she doth of sorrow speak,
E'en from my heart the strings do break.

There underlay, however, the spontaneous delight with which poetry was preoccupied a rougher seriousness, that in the next century was to become predominant. Continual pleasure tires, and since it was always the Elizabethan lyricists intention to please, their work naturally incited a reaction. There is a greater music than that of the nightingales, and it may be heard in the poetry of Sir Walter Ralegh (*c.* 1552–1618). His admonition to his soul, in his poem *The Lie*, gives the profound and moving note which he sounded:

> *Go, soul, the body's guest,*
> *Upon a thankless arrant;*
> *Fear not to touch the best;*
> *The truth shall be thy warrant.*
> *Go, since I needs must die,*
> *And give the world the lie.*

The critical examination to which poetry can submit the world had been overlooked, but Ralegh, among others, recalled it to that duty.

The great Elizabethan poets, Samuel Daniel (*c.* 1563-1619), Michael Drayton (1563-1631), Edmund Spenser, and William Shakespeare (1564-1616)—who surpasses all poets as the world exceeds the largest continent—knit up in their work every poetic strand with which the lesser poets had been separately concerned, and they effortlessly adopted any form that they needed. Each wrote remarkable sonnet sequences, in which they subtly analysed their emotion and memorialized their love with boasts as proud as that of Daniel:

> *When winter snows upon thy sable hairs,*
> *And frost of age hath nipped thy beauties near;*
> *When dark shall seem thy day that never clears,*
> *And all lies withered that was held so dear;*
> *Then take this picture which I here present thee,*
> *Limned with a pencil not all unworthy;*
> *Here see the gifts that God and Nature lent thee;*
> *Here read thyself, and what I suffered for thee.*
> *This may remain thy lasting monument,*
> *Which happily posterity may cherish;*
> *These colours with thy fading are not spent;*
> *These may remain when thou and I shall perish.*
> *If they remain, then thou shalt live thereby;*
> *They will remain, and so thou canst not die.*

Each wrote songs and pastorals, which lightly or profoundly moved from love to death, from humour to philosophy; and each separately seems to comprise in his works the whole of poetry.

This was the age of opulence, and the poets squandered their new-found wealth as extravagantly as if they knew it to be inexhaustible. Such a time can never recur—at least, not until men alight on the stars and rejuvenate the imagination by their discoveries—it is, like their favourite Phœnix, unique.

WORKING MEN'S COLLEGE LIBRARY

IX

THEATRE

J. C. TREWIN

EW that saw a production of Shakespeare's *King
Lear* at Stratford-upon-Avon in 1936 and 1937—it
was by a Russian producer, Theodore Komisarjev-
sky—will have forgotten the ceremonial raising of the
gold trumpets. These gleamed suddenly on either side of
the great staircase where Lear sat enthroned. First a shine
of gold, then a lifting—almost as of a wind-stirred group
of daffodils—and at last the flourish, the mingled voice.
The coming of the Elizabethan drama was like that: a
slow rising followed by a quick blaze of colour and sound
comparable with the speaking of the Abbey trumpets on
Coronation Day. Was not this, indeed, the Coronation Day
of the English theatre—brought newly from the dark?

Before the first years of Elizabeth's reign English
drama, which had its beginnings in the liturgy of the
Church, had stirred only in the ancient Mystery and
Miracle plays of the craft guilds and, later, in the more
allegorical Moralities, full of personified abstractions—
Good Deeds, Beauty, and so forth—and the brisker comic
Interludes. One of these, a play called, briefly, *Fulgens*

*and Lucres,** by Henry Medwall, was not re-discovered until 1919.

What, first, were the Miracles and Mysteries? What would you have seen if you had stood in a crowd at, say, Coventry or Hull or York on a Corpus Christi Day during the fifteenth and early sixteenth centuries? There would have passed you, or—if you had a fortunate stand—stopped in front of you, a kind of travelling, two-tiered stage, built on a six-wheeled cart known as a 'pageant'. A sixteenth-century record describes it as 'an highe place made like an howse, with two rowmes being open on the top; in the lower rowme they apparelled and dressed themselves; and in the higher rowme they played, and they stood upon wheels'. Upon this wagon you would have seen a lively representation of some scriptural tale, or fragment from the life of a saint. Hell's Mouth might be gaping, or Noah's wife would scold. There was often a long procession of 'pageants', so that you might have had an entire Biblical sequence, each group taking a different incident. Effects could be elaborate. Thus in one play of *St. Mary Magdalene* there was a 'stage and Hell ondyr-neth that stage'; the Chelmsford accounts speak of 'fiftie fadam of lyne for the clowdes', and else-where we have such a charming property-note as 'a link to set the world on fire'. Costumes were equally lavish. A detailed Norwich inventory includes 'a cote with hosen and tayle for ye serpente steyned'. Coventry records (1544) speak of 'a new coat and a pair of hose for Gabriel', and somewhere else there is an entry about 'two yards and a half of buckram for the Holy Ghost's coat'.

The actors who stood on the pageants, so carefully

*Its full title was *A godely Interlude of Fulgens Cenatoure of Rome and Lucres his Daughter.*

contrived, were rough, vigorous players matched to their plays. All would be members of the local craft guilds—the Shipwrights, maybe, or the Cappers, the Plasterers, or the Drapers, or the Cordwainers. Their plays were in the vernacular, with a good deal of racketing comedy as well as passages of high seriousness, devised clumsily enough but with a kind of crystalline purity. All was fresh, eager, confident: the crowds would accept the efforts of their craft-actors in a properly mingled spirit of laughter and devotion.

The Moralities, much later in growth, were larger, more ambitious, more didactic, less charade-like than the Mysteries and Miracles. Here there was a blossoming of theatrical forms; often, as in *Everyman* (c. 1495) by an unknown author, a clear poetic glow. Professional actors were coming in now; the strolling players—first in a long fellowship of English touring companies—who went upon the road as a natural development of the professional entertainers of the Middle Ages. They would perform anywhere they could get a hearing—observe the origin of 'barnstorming'—but those especially fortunate might find a stage in some gentleman's hall, and (as the years passed) the luckiest might even become members of a private troop of players under direct noble patronage.

The rough little Interludes, which appeared at the beginning of the sixteenth century and grew in popularity, moved away from wholly religious themes to the secular. You looked no longer upon the play as a semi-religious rite. When, in Henry VIII's reign, you went to *A Mery Play between the Pardoner and the Frere, the Curate and Neybour Pratte,** or to the same author's *The Playe Called the Foure P.P.*, with its famous lines:

*By John Heywood (?1497–1587).

120

I never saw nor knew in my consyens
Any one woman out of paciens . . .

you went primarily to laugh, not to be edified. At this
time the professional actor—neither the craftsman nor
the gentleman-amateur nor the Thespian choirboy—
was technically in the rogue-and-vagabond-and-Sturdy-
Beggar class. The stage was only a poor profession unless
you were nominally under some noble patronage and, as
one of 'the Duke's servants', wearing his livery, kept out
of the eye of the law. It was an eye that, by 1572, looked
frowningly upon all unlicensed 'Fencers, Bearewardes,
Common Players in Enterludes and Minstrels, not
belonging to any Baron of this Realme or other honourable personage of greater degree'. From these struggling
actors, their shifts and their stratagems and their inn-
yard adventuring, rose at last the companies that were to
make the aspiring music of the Elizabethan spring. You
will find, by the way, an uncommonly vivid Tudor
domestic picture in Act Four of *The Booke of Sir Thomas
More,* an anonymous Elizabethan play with one speech
in it thought now to be by Shakespeare himself. In the
fourth act the Lord Cardinal's Players—that is, the
players attached to the household of Wolsey—act before
More and his guests at a Chelsea banquet. The First
Player runs through the titles in his repertory (they include Heywood's *The Play of Four Ps*) and More makes
his choice:

The Marriage of Wit and Wisdom! *that, my lads;*
I'll none but that; the theme is very good,
And may maintain a liberal argument . . .

We are then shown the full performance—and a lively
business and 'liberal argument' it is.

By the middle of the sixteenth century drama in England was shaping itself. Your great-grandfather and grandfather would have seen the guild-players in street or square. Your father, if he had been privileged, would have watched one of the early interludes in a gentleman's hall, or else he might have joined the ring about the strolling players in some remote village. Now you yourself, with your friends, were crowding a quadrangular, galleried inn-yard (possibly that at Gloucester, still surviving) to hear the actors romp through one of the newer, more elaborate pieces from the height of their trestle-borne scaffold.

At first there was nothing very much to hear. The early verse was simple, the kind of bumpy, bucketing, crudely-rhymed stuff that we meet now in pantomime. You will find it in such comedies of historic note as *Ralph Roister Doister,* by Nicholas Udall (1505–1556), headmaster in his day of both Eton and Westminster, and *Gammer Gurton's Needle,* by 'Mr. S.', an unknown author—maybe William Stevenson of Cambridge—who wrote in the mid-century. Here are two lines from *Gammer Gurton*:

> *Might ha' kept it when ye had it! but fools will*
> *be fools still.*
> *Lose that is vast in your hands? Ye need not, but*
> *ye will.*

These plays had two derivations, native and classical. Their dramatists were trying to add to the bumbling interlude-matter something of the craftsmanship of the classical comedies of Terence. The native tradition produced a lively enthusiasm, the raciness of what has been called the 'elementary, mother-wit stage'. The Latin influence strengthened construction and character. In tragedy Seneca, a Roman dramatist of the first century, was the model. Tragedies had to be formal in design, with a good deal of dull chronicling on stage and much sanguinary incident off. Dramatic blank verse, as it appeared at last in a key-play, the neo-Senecan, academic-aristocratic tragedy of *Gorboduc*, by Thomas Sackville (Lord Buckhurst) and Thomas Norton, in January 1562, was a plain without perceptible hills, a stately drone without variation of accent. Thus:

> *Did ever age bring forth such tyrant hearts?*
> *The brother hath bereft the brother's life,*
> *The mother, she hath dyed her cruel hands*
> *In blood of her own son; and now at last*
> *The people, lo, forgetting truth and love,*
> *Contemning quite both law and loyal heart,*
> *Ev'n they have slain their sovereign lord and*
>   *Queen.*

It was a beginning. A more popular theatre was rising now, a theatre of action. Besides the dignified neo-classical men, writing for Court performance, there were dramatists with a genuinely common touch, ready at a word to turn out sprawling, crowded mythological pieces, or historical chronicles launched upon a swelling tide of Elizabethan patriotism. Drama, too, had caught the tide—one that brought the players from the inn-yards to the new theatres of London based upon the inn-yard model, with courtyards that were circular instead of square. There, upon a rush-strewn platform-stage thrust into the middle of his audience and half-open to the sky, an Elizabethan actor could strut and declaim and, so we are led to believe, act more excitingly than the theatre had ever known or has known since.

What was this stage like? James Burbage, who had been leader of a nobleman's company, Leicester's Men, built (in 1576) the first English playhouse, called simply The Theatre, a wooden erection in Shoreditch. Others followed, at first—by illiberal decree—without the City bounds. There was an open courtyard, surrounded by three galleried tiers, the 'wooden O'. A wide stage—Shakespeare's 'unworthy scaffold'—jutted into the centre of the courtyard, covered partly by a roof or 'shadowe' supported on columns. At the back, recessed between entrances, there was a curtained inner stage, and above this again a balcony. Juliet's tomb, for instance, might be on the inner stage; earlier she would have spoken from the balcony her share of the love-duet with Romeo. The audience pressed thickly about the platform during the two hours' traffic of the play. Actors were not separated as they are to-day, isolated from their hearers behind a picture-frame. Then they stood and delivered in the very middle of a crowd that packed urgently around (some favoured folk on the stage itself) and listened with a strong, emotional appreciation unaffected by the intermittent cracking of nuts and an occasional draught of bottle-ale.

Actors wore the usual Elizabethan costume with a few distinctive additions such as a sash or a Roman breastplate. Boys played all the female roles. There was no scenery, and it was left to the dramatist to paint the scene in words—Shakespeare became an adept at this—and to indicate promptly any change of place. ('A goodly city is this Antium.') On the other hand the actors had a store of properties. The 1598 inventory of that shrewd theatre manager, Philip Henslowe, names 'one tree of Gowelden apelles, Tantelouse tre', 'one rocke, one cage, one tomb, one Hell mought', 'one gowelden fleece; two rackets; one baye tree', and so on.

The Elizabethan age, during which the drama began to flourish so excitingly, was eager, passionate, adventurous. A noise of far-off seas beat through London's narrow ways. The world was expanding. Sailors brought home news from the realms of gold. It was a time of sultry splendours and frigid cruelties, one of brave words tossed about like handfuls of gold pieces or spun back and forth like tennis-balls. Plainly dramas of this English Renaissance must be in the grand manner, a royal, prodigal, incandescent manner. Soon the hour brought the man. A year or so before Medina Sidonia's Armada—seen from the cliffs of the Lizard—surged up Channel in its broad half-moon, London heard the voice of Christopher Marlowe (1564–1593), graduate of Cambridge, son of a Canterbury cobbler. He was the poet of 'brave, translunary things': in his hand the ten-syllabled iambic line, unrhymed, became a new and remarkable instrument. Verse that had smouldered sulkily began to flame.

Other authors, for instance Thomas Kyd (1558–1594), who wrote *The Spanish Tragedy*, could put together a serviceable piece of storm-along melodrama:

> *Tragedia cothurnata, fitting kings,*
> *Containing matter, and not common things,*

but none had Marlowe's transforming voice. What John Lyly (1544–1606), another of the coterie of University Wits, was doing for prose comedy—Lyly, writing for boy players, was master of the courtly-fantastic, the gossamer conceit—Marlowe did for blank verse drama. His were the 'high, astounding terms', the ride in triumph through Persepolis, the 'almond tree y-mounted high', the 'fiery, spangled veil of heaven', the 'sweet fruition of an earthly crown'. It was heady stuff, and it went to the heads of its listeners. Everything seemed larger than life-size in that daybreak when Marlowe, as Swinburne wrote 300 years later in exultant homage, came

> *Crowned, girdled, garbed and shod with light and*
> *fire,*
> *Son first-born of the morning, sovereign star.*

His chief plays were—as a matter of record—the two parts of *Tamburlaine the Great, Dr. Faustus, The Jew of Malta, Edward the Second*. Of these *Tamburlaine* was the most resounding; *Faustus*—a valley between two peaks—contained matchless poetry, including the apostrophe to Helen ('O she is fairer than the evening air'); and *Edward the Second,* which Shakespeare must have had in mind when he wrote *Richard the Second* a few years later, was the most complete artistic achievement.

The Elizabethan 'eighties and 'nineties brought other playwrights high in the dawn-chorus of University Wits: Robert Greene (1558–1592) and George Peele (1558–1597). Each could build the lofty rhyme, and we forget neither Greene's

> *Why, thinks King Henry's son that Margaret's*
> *love*
> *Hangs in the uncertain balance of proud time?*
> *That death shall make a discord of our thoughts?*

nor Peele's

> *She that in chains of pearl and unicorn*
> *Leads at her train the ancient golden world.*

But, after Marlowe lay dead in a Deptford tavern,

stabbed by the dagger of one Ingram Frizer, a greater than he or his fellows moved to the head of the Elizabethan theatre. William Shakespeare (1564–1616), actor of Stratford-upon-Avon birth, had a wider range than the 'dead shepherd' he lamented. To Marlowe's drum, trumpet, and fife he brought the lutes, the gradual violins, the soft recorders. He orchestrated English blank verse as no one before him had done or would do again. Tragedy, farce, romance, high comedy, chronicle—here was all the stuff of the Elizabethan stage, the borrowings from Holinshed and Plutarch and the romantic story-tellers, every accepted device employed and transformed with a superlative art. Beside his 'vast sea' even the best of Tudor and Stuart dramatists—Marlowe, Jonson, and Webster apart—can glimmer only as 'the morn-dew on the myrtle-leaf'.

There were many sharers in the drama's age of gold. Where, hardly half a century before, tragedians and raw farceurs were still committing horrors with a blunt instrument, the stage held now the high procession of Ben Jonson, master-builder of what he called the Comedy of Humours; Webster, Dekker, Massinger, Ford, Chapman, Beaumont and Fletcher, and others whose place is in a later article. Shakespeare who, with *Hamlet* (1601), had reached his zenith not long before the time (the end of Elizabeth's reign) when this section must end, easily surpassed his rivals. Ben Jonson hailed him after death as

Soul of the Age!
The applause! delight! the wonder of our stage!

From our own day let me borrow the words of John Masefield, the Poet Laureate, upon *Hamlet*: 'The great, wise, and wonderful beauty of the play is a part of the

127

English mind for ever'. So we might say of the entire First Folio of 1623: the plays done at their zenith by the King's Men, led by Richard Burbage (son of James) and by the great comedian, Kempe.

The Elizabethan stage, of which Shakespeare was at the core, held the true spirit of its period—one that lasted, in effect, until well into the reign of James I. It is wrong to prettify the Elizabethans, to present them as something gay and newly-laundered, with a Wardour Street swagger under the olde oake beames. The plays blow away this nonsense. When we open the pages (or, better, see them acted), with their huddling tragedy and farce, their strange juxtapositions, their verse that takes mind and heart, we may meet with either a gust of wind that jerks our heads back, or with a sulphur-charged world before storm. This drama is indeed the sound and semblance of its age: gallant, lusty, lustful, proud, tigerish, courtly—the epithets stream on. Academic scholarship, with its rightful and valuable insistence on dates, quartos, folios, and the rest, sometimes blurs for us the sheer *excitement* of a time when a sharply responsive audience crowded about the platform, when every topical sally made its mark, and when the Bastard Faulconbridge's 'Come the three corners' and the declamation of Henry V would strike sparks from every hearer. No matter if the stage were bare. The theatres—the Curtain or the Swan or the Rose, the Fortune or the Hope or the Bankside's Globe—could hold all the kingdoms of the known world. The Elizabethans were lords of language. They wrote in words that now flamed, now came in 'like starlight, hid with jewels' (that is Jonson in *Volpone*). An Irishman, Seán O'Casey, has something of that gift to-day. They would, I think, have known his

WORKING MEN'S
COLLEGE
LIBRARY

The picture here set down
within this letter T,
Aright doth shew the forme
of Tharlton vnto the shap.
When hee in pleasaunt wise,
the Countenance exprest
of Clowne to cote of russet,
and sturtups to v reste, hew.

Whoe merry many made,
when he appeard in sight
The graue and wise as well as
at him did take delight truth,

The partie nowe is gone,
and closlie clad in claye,
Of all the Iesters in the land,
he bare the praise awaie.

Now hath he plaid his pte,
and sure he is of this.
If him Christe did dieto liue,
with him in lasting blis.

TARLTON AS A CLOWN
from an Elizabethan Alphabet Book

THE VISIT OF QUEEN ELIZABETH TO BLACKFRIARS, 16th JUNE, 1600

quality on Bankside when dramatists walked the stage in kingly-flashing coats and a relatively minor writer, Thomas Dekker, in the minor play of *Old Fortunatus*, could toss off such lines as these:

> *Behold yon town, there stands mine armoury,*
> *In which are corselets forged of beaten gold,*
> *To arm ten hundred thousand fighting men,*
> *Whose glittering squadrons when the sun beholds,*
> *They seem like to ten hundred thousand Joves,*
> *When Jove on the proud back of thunder rides,*
> *Trapped all in lightning flames: there can I*
> *show thee*
> *The ball of gold that set all Troy on fire . . .*

Rather the plays of gold that set all Thames on fire. That light was, alas, to wane and die in the thinner airs of Charles I's reign. But the Elizabethans are with us yet. Where, after three hundred and fifty years, are their successors? Where the Promethean heat that can their light relume?

I

X

PROSE LITERATURE

GILBERT PHELPS

'The inseparability of the word and the thing is . . . in one form or another, the postulate of all positive cultural epochs.'—WILBUR MARSHALL URBAN in *Language and Reality*.

WHEN we turn to the Tudor period in English literature we usually think of the great flowering of lyric and dramatic poetry. But the advance of English prose was if anything even more surprising, and in its implications for our culture just as important. By the turn of the century it could show solid achievements in narrative and description, in burlesque, and 'poetical' prose, in literary criticism, in philosophy and in theology. The pamphleteers, and in particular Nashe, had hammered out a highly effective satirical style, and pointed the way to Swift, Johnson, and ultimately to Joyce. The journalists had evolved a style of realistic reporting, and anticipated Defoe. The short-story writers and novelists had laid the foundations of the eighteenth-century novel, and the translation of the Bibles, made by Tyndale, Miles Coverdale and their

successors, had provided the basis for the Authorized
Version of 1611.

The transformation seems even more spectacular when
we remember the great prestige of Latin as the medium for
serious expression, and the uncertainty and poverty of
written English prose before, say, 1560. Poetry and the
drama had already established an English tradition, but
prose had to start from scratch, and it was a long time
before the position of Latin was seriously shaken. The early
Humanists on the whole avoided English—Sir Thomas
More's *Utopia,* for example, was in the first instance
written in Latin, and as late as 1620 Bacon would entrust
his most serious work, the *Instauratio Magna*, only to
Latin.

Even when the Humanists did use English they regarded it as a second-best. Roger Ascham (1515–1568)
in his preface to *Toxophilus* (1545) admitted that it would
have been 'more honest for my name' to have written in
Latin, but, as his purpose is an educational one, he uses
English to 'further the pleasure or commoditie of the
gentlemen and yeomen of England'. His style, however,
is as close to the Latin as he can make it, modelled in
particular upon Cicero and Seneca.

The educational aims of the Humanists did, however,
lend a considerable impetus to the development of
English prose, and many of them in spite of themselves
wrote fluently and simply in English. The English translation of More's *Utopia* made in 1557 is admirable
prose. *The Heart of Sedition* by Sir John Cheke (1514–
1557) which was directed against the Norfolk rebels (and
which incidentally set the 'tone' of Elizabethan utterances on rebellion) is vigorous and eloquent, and
frequently homely and humorous. There is fine prose too

in Sir Thomas Elyot (1490–1546) and Sir Thomas Wilson (1525–1581) recommends, and sometimes practises, 'purity' of language and the avoidance of 'inkhorn terms' and 'outlandish Englische'. Even Ascham is still decidedly readable and not only because in *The Scholemaster* he proved himself to be our first important educationist.

Curiously enough, however, it was the 'mediævalists' rather than the Humanists who at this stage did the most important work in English prose. In 1484 Caxton's new printing press had produced the famous *Morte d'Arthur* of Sir Thomas Malory (*c.* 1430–1470). Malory claimed to have translated from a French book, but it seems clear that in fact he exploited many sources, oral as well as written, and his great achievement was to make a prose romance out of a chaotic mass of history and legend that had been accumulating for centuries. For this work he evolved a style which was deliberately archaic, turning back to the earlier Middle Ages not only for vocabulary but frequently for its rhythms and intonations, but which in passages of narration and description was vivid and beautiful. Moreover the *Morte d'Arthur*, in spite of its muddled structure, and its equally muddled morality (which earned a sharp reproof from Ascham), has an impressive unity of atmosphere. It is a curious, nostalgic atmosphere, reminding one in its wistful yearning for an idealized past of *Piers Plowman*.

The position of Caxton, the printer of the *Morte d'Arthur*, is a paradoxical one. The introduction of the printing press inevitably contributed to the development of English prose, and ultimately to the Reformation. He himself did a good deal for the 'purification' of English prose. But the immediate results of the work of Caxton, and of his successors—Wynkyn de Worde, Richard

Pinson and others—was to provide the English public with books that pointed backwards to the past rather than forward to the Renaissance. In spite of their 'mediæ-valism', however, the romances of Malory, Lord Berners (1467-1533) and others which came from the new printing presses—and especially (it is significant to note) during the Catholic 'interregnum' of Mary Tudor's reign, had a far-reaching influence. The persistency of the tradition is remarkable: the end of the process is to be seen in the chap-books of the eighteenth century when the stories originally invented for knights and ladies, end in the penny tracts of *Guy of Warwick, Bevis of Hampton,* and *The Seven Wise Masters*—and their indirect influence even then was not exhausted.

In other words, English prose from its beginnings was subjected to the influence of mediæval romance as well as to that of the new forces of the Renaissance.

Far more powerful than Humanism or Romance in establishing English prose was the over-riding desire of the religious reformers to appeal direct to the people. The translators of the Bible set out to write lucid and idiomatic prose that would suit every social level and they carefully avoided affectations of style. At the same time the subject-matter imposed dignity and restraint, while the rhythms of the original Hebrew came through in the translations. The result was an amalgam—a prose style that lay between poetry and popular speech: it was the quintessence of the various processes that went to the evolution of English culture.

The influence of the Bible, and of the Book of Common Prayer (which was issued by Archbishop Cranmer in 1549), was of course to prove enormous. Sunday after Sunday the people of England listened to them until the national consciousness was permeated with their rhythms and idiom. It was so pervasive an influence that before long it was itself modifying popular usage. But it was a two-way process, for it must never be forgotten that English Biblical prose derived much of its vigour and vitality from 'The language really used by men', and the strength of the Biblical tradition lies in this firm rooting in English soil.

This affinity with folk language is demonstrated when we turn to the utterances of reformers who were engaged in less exacting tasks than the rendering into English of the Word of God—and in particular to the popular preachers. In the sermons of Hugh Latimer, for example (1485–1555), we can find in profusion the turns of phrase, the proverbial expressions, the idioms of the countryside and the market-place which, used with more conscious artistic control by the translators of the Bible lend strength and vitality to their style.

At the opposite pole to the prose in intention of Latimer's sermons was the rough and ready prose of the Tudor Jest-Books—but in fact they belong to the same tradition. These Jest Books are obviously based on an oral tradition, though in form they frequently follow the mediæval 'exempla', and in manner they follow on from the 'fabliaux' and Chaucer. *The Hundred Merry Tales* (1528) and *The Sackful of Newes* (1557) are pretty clearly derived from popular sources; *Merry Tales, Witty Questions and Quick Answers* are mainly borrowed from literary sources; but the collectors soon began to ascribe their anecdotes to individuals—hence *Scogin's Jests* in 1565, Dr. Skelton's in 1567.

A study of these old Jest Books drives home the important realization that in Tudor times—as in all 'positive cultural epochs'—there is, lying behind the prose of the scholars and 'the literary gentlemen', that 'other language' of buying and selling, ploughing, harvesting, and carting, and that the vitality of literature leaps or flickers according to the reality of its contact with that energizing source. And the humble Jest Books in the long run probably had a far more lasting influence on English creative prose that the 'poetical' prose of Malory or the *than* pedantic prose of the scholars.

Even before the Renaissance began fully to take effect, then, English prose exhibited many of its typical tendencies. There was first of all the opposition between Realism and Romance—mediævalism on the one hand and the jest-book tradition on the other: there were the impulses provided by the scholars and the Humanists, and by the translators of the Bible, and to these might be added the further impetus of a growing nationalism. The Chroniclers of the earlier period—Edward Hall (1497?–1547), Ralph Holinshed, whose *Chronicle* was published in 1578, and John Stow (born *c.* 1525) belong to the same patriotic tradition as the famous *Principall Navigations, Voiages, and Discoveries* of Richard Hakluyt (1553–1616).

The next stage, however, belongs to the translators. Between 1560 and 1600 no less than 68 Greek works were translated into English, and versions from the Latin were equally numerous. For the most part, though, the English translators were not scholars who worked from the original texts. Philemon Holland, with his careful versions of Livy, Pliny the Elder, and Suetonius was one of the few exceptions. Most of them drew on French and Italian sources, but the results were in many cases themselves works of creative imagination. The most famous of all the translations from the Classics was of course Sir Thomas North's translation of *Plutarch's Lives* (1579) which was based upon the French text by Amyot, but which was written in fine lucid and idiomatic English. Next to the Bible, North's Plutarch probably had more influence on 'literary' English of the Tudor and Jacobean periods than any other single book.

The translators soon turned to contemporary literatures. Important and influential translations were made from the French and the Spanish—notably Anthony Munday's translations of the Spanish chivalrous romances and of Montemayor's *Diana* (all made before the end of the sixteenth century), and John Florio's *Montaigne* (1603).

It was Italy and Italian culture, however, that made the most powerful impression on the English imagination—an attraction made all the more exciting because it was compounded of revulsion and fascination. One of the most important translations from the Italian was that made by Thomas Hoby in 1561 of the famous handbook of Renaissance manners—Castiglione's *Il Cortegiano*, which was one of the major influences in the work of Sir Philip Sidney.

Even more important in the long run were the Italian 'novelle', though at this stage the treatment they received from the English translators related them to the same 'courtly' tradition as that represented by *Il Cortegiano* and Sidney. The earliest 'novella' to be rendered into English was a version of one of Boccaccio's tales included, under the title of *Titus and Gisippus*, in *The Governour* of Sir Thomas Elyot (1490–1546).

There is evidence to suggest that Elyot's style had some

influence on William Painter (1540–1594), the first great Tudor collector of short stories. His *Palace of Pleasure* (1566–1567) contained 101 tales, most of them derived from the Italian 'novella' writers—Boccaccio, Cinthio, Bandello, Straparola, Masuccio, and Sei Giovanni Fiorentino.

Painter's attitude towards his Italian material is typical of the divided English conscience. He revels in the sensuousness of the tales, but is at pains to stress that his avowed aim is to teach ethics. This ambivalence of mood is even more apparent in the work of Sir George Fenton (1539–1608), communicating to his prose a tension which is often most effective. Moreover, he brings us a step closer to euphuism, for his translations of Bandello's tales were taken at second hand from the French writer Belleforest. Now Belleforest had transformed the easy Italian of his original into a stiffly brocaded pattern, introducing numerous set pieces, and elaborate ethical commentaries, all in a high-flown and highly ornamental style.

Then in 1576 George Pettie (1548–1589), in a collection of tales called *A Petite Palace of Pettie his Pleasures,* carried the process a stage farther, so that when John Lyly (1554–1606) came to write his famous *Euphues* the elements of the euphuistic style were already present in varying degree in the work of Painter, Fenton, and Pettie. But in the two parts of *Euphues* (*Euphues, or the Anatomy of Wit* in 1578, and *Euphues his England* in 1580) Lyly built up the stylistic devices already practised into a deliberate system.

As an illustration of the euphuistic style I have an affection for the following reply by a lady to her lover's suit, chiefly because of its unconscious irony—

'Gentle-man, a short sute is soone made, but great

matters not easily graunted; if your request be reasonable, wil serve, if not, a thousand wil not suffice. Therefore if ther be anything that I may do you pleasure in, see it be honest, and use not tedious discourses, or colours of Rhetoricke, which though they may be thoughte courtly, yet are they not esteemed necessary: for the purest Emerauld shineth brightest when it hath no oyle, and truth delighteth best, when it is apparayled worst.'

Euphuism as moulded by Lyly actually contains two distinct elements. In the first place there is the principle of counterpoise and symmetry in sentences and clauses, together with an elaborate overlay of alliteration, and often double or crossed alliteration, as in 'Gentle-*m*an, a *s*hort *s*ute is *s*oone *m*ade, but *g*reat *m*atters not easily graunted', where 'g's', 'm's', and 's's' are all elaborately arranged.

The second principle of euphuism is the use of embellishment of all kinds of images, metaphors, and illustrations drawn from mythology, and ancient history, and above all from that odd natural history which is to be found in the mediæval and early Tudor bestiaries, herbaries, lapidaries, etc. The emerald 'that hath no oyle' in the above passage is typical.

Closely associated with *Euphues* in stylistic tendencies is *The Arcadia* of Sir Philip Sidney (1554–1586). Between them these two works set the standard for 'fine writing' in the Elizabethan period and beyond. They were followed by a host of imitators, the most considerable of whom was Robert Greene (1560–1592), whose *Mamilia* was closely modelled on *Euphues*, and who produced several romances in the manner of *Arcadia*.

At first sight it seems odd that English prose, which had shown so much promise of variety and flexibility should have run into this blind alley. But there are many contributory factors that help to explain the pheno-menon. From the strictly literary point of view Painter, Pettie, and Fenton through Belleforest had already begun the process. The Spanish writer Guevara, who was first translated by Lord Berners (1467–1533—the translator also of Froissart's *Chronicle*), is said to have influenced the texture of Lyly's style. More important probably was the influence of Latin prose style, particularly of Cicero and Seneca: in fact Ascham's prose, with its symmetrical, balanced and antithetic sentences, admittedly modelled on Seneca, had long before pointed the way to euphuism. To this influence too might possibly be added that of the well-remembered rhythms of mediæval plain-song.

The chief significance, however, of this phase in English prose is that it reflects the prevailing mood of the courtiers in Tudor England, who at the same time that they were excited by the intellectual and physical adven-tures of the Renaissance, were also aware of its threat to the old order to which they belonged, and so retreated behind the barriers of stylization and convention. This 'escapist' tendency is of course particularly obvious in Sidney's *Arcadia*, with its kinship to Malory's *Morte d'Arthur*.

Not that the effect of Lyly's and Sidney's work was entirely retrogressive. There is some effective satire in the first part of *Euphues*, and the euphuistic style itself did a service to prose at a time when it was necessary to bring form to the formless, and to set positive standards of artistry. At times Sidney in *The Arcadia* writes magni-ficently—*The Paphlagonian Unkind King*, for example (which is one of the sources of *King Lear*), is one of the finest of the Elizabethan short stories. Sidney's elaborations on human emotion and behaviour too, marked a real advance in characterization, and pointed forward to the 'conceits' of the Metaphysicals and to the sentimental refinements of Richardson. Moreover the euphuistic and courtly styles were not entirely specialist in their appeal: form and regularity had an attraction for the Tudor mind, in spite of the general exuberance of its activities, and I think that a thorough examination of *euphuism* would demand some consideration of the Elizabethan 'Concept of Order'.

Nevertheless if English prose had not advanced beyond this stage it would have died of suffocation. But the forces of Realism were more powerful than those of courtly Romance and mediævalism. To begin with, the diversion of the Italian 'novella' into the channels that lead to euphuism was achieved only by violence. In temper and atmosphere it belonged more naturally to the realistic tradition.

Throughout the period the 'novella' became increasingly popular, and its complete domestication was symbolized by *A Pleasant Fable of Ferdinando Jeronimi and Leonora de Velasco* which George Gascoigne (*c.* 1525–1577) included in his *Hundred Sundrie Flowers* in 1572: this tale pretended to be a translation from a mythical Italian named Bartello, but was in actual fact Gascoigne's own work.

Included in this original English 'novella' is the tale of Mistress Frances, her elderly husband and her young lover. It is the first really successful original short story in this deliberate Italian Renaissance tradition. The plot is reminiscent of Boccaccio; the telling is fresh and vivid in the manner of Chaucer.

Other followers of the Italian 'novella' produced fine

work, and notably Barnabe Riche (*c.* 1540–1617), whose most interesting work is his *Farewell to the Military Profession* (1581), a collection of eight tales mainly from Italian sources. One of them—*Apolonius and Silla*—brings to Elizabethan fiction a new romantic charm, gaiety and lightness of touch, as well as some excellent dialogue and easy narration. Shakespeare's *Twelfth Night* derived charm of atmosphere as well as plot from this tale. Robert Greene's *Roberto's Tale* from his *Groatsworth of Wit* is another typical example of the Anglicized 'novella'.

At the same time the popular tradition of story-telling maintained its vigour. The vogue of the Jest Books continued, and many new collections appeared, for example *Tarlton's News out of Purgatrie, The Cobbler of Canterbury* and *Westward for Smelts,* all published after 1590. Moreover, a most significant dovelopment took place in the Jest Books. For the anecdotes were increasingly centred upon a particular character, so that in 1582 we have *Long Meg of Westminster,* about 1594 *The Famous History of Fryer Bacon,* and about 1587 *The History of Doctor Faustus*. The titles themselves strongly suggest that the Jest Book was rapidly becoming the 'Life and Adventures' of a picaresque hero.

It is indeed most important to realize that side by side with the literature of Arcadia ran this other literature of the tavern, the market-place and the brothel. It is the tradition drawn upon by Shakespeare in his creation of Falstaff, and it is the tradition of English realistic fiction. In the long run, therefore, the most important event in the history of Elizabethan creative prose was not the appearance of the 'poetical' prose of *Euphues* and *Arcadia* but the meeting of the Italian 'novella' and the

English Jest Book to lay the foundations of the English Realistic Novel.

The high-water mark of the process in Elizabethan fiction is marked by Thomas Deloney (1543?–1600?), who in his novels of Elizabethan bourgeois life—*Jacke of Newbury, The Gentle Craft,* and *Thomas of Reading*—blended the various elements in Elizabethan prose to form a supple and racy narrative style. He is very close to the world of the Jest Books, in atmosphere as well as in idiom. The story of Richard Casteler in *The Gentle Craft* with its debt to *Long Meg of Westminster* is an especially striking example.

Deloney is of great importance in any study of the English Novel, but the first symptoms of the new realistic impulse are to be found in that curious fugitive pamphlet journalism devoted to the study of the Tudor under-world. The pioneers in this field were John Awdeley with his *Fraternity of Vagabonds* (1560), and Thomas Harman and his *Caveat to Common Cursitors* (1567), and the impulse reached its culmination in the 'coney-catching' pamphlets of Robert Greene—*The Notable Discoverie of Cosenage* (1591) and the *Defence of Coney Catching* in 1592. *The Alarm to Usurers* by Thomas Lodge (*c.* 1558–1625), the author of the fine romance *Rosalynde,* is in the same tradition.

The aim of these writers was ostensibly a moral one, but they threw themselves into the depiction of low life with such gusto, and with such loving attention to all the details of roguery, including thieves' jargon, that one cannot but presume a sneaking sympathy. Embedded in their tracts were many anecdotes which are often authentic short stories. This literature of vagabondage, joining forces with that of the Jest Books, did in fact inaugurate the great line of English fiction whose culminating achievements are *Moll Flanders, Tom Jones,* and *Humphrey Clinker.*

The excitement of investigation, moreover, produced some of the most characteristic Elizabethan prose—vivid, colourful, idiomatic, full of body and pace, and the same qualities emerged in the more serious pamphlets of the period, heightened by the addition of religious and partisan motives. Elizabethan prose was perhaps most at home in invective, and the Martin Marprelate controversy between the Puritans and the Anglicans (1588–1593) provided an excellent battleground. The leading Martinists were hanged in 1593; the most vigorous of the Anglican champions was Thomas Nashe (1567–1601).

Now Nashe is undoubtedly one of our greatest prose writers. It is not only that in *The Unfortunate Traveller, or the Life of Jacke Wilton* (1594) he produced the first English picaresque novel, or that in his various books he wrote superb short stories, it is above all that he used to the full all the resources of Elizabethan prose. In narrative and in invective his control of tempo, and his emotional range are amazing. In works such as *The Anatomie of Absurditie* (1589), *Pierce Penilesse and his Supplication to the Divill* (1592) and *Christ's Tears over Jereusalem* (1593) he evolves a highly seasoned personal style. His realism is unflinching, and he communicates his horrors of torture, plague and rape in a deceptively matter-of-fact, and even flippant, tone which is terrible in its cumulative satirical effect, and which is comparable to that of Swift's *Modest Proposal.*

*   *   *   *

A study of Tudor prose ends appropriately with Nashe.

It would be possible of course to follow the same impulses into the Stuart period. Much Jacobean prose is fundamentally Elizabethan, and writers like Dekker, Raleigh, Bacon, and Milton belong to both periods. All the same, there was a distinctively Jacobean prose, just as there was a Jacobean architecture—and the 'baroque' is perhaps symptomatic of them both. The death of Queen Elizabeth did roughly coincide with the end of a prose era, and it is to the Stuart period that the developments leading to so-called 'modern prose' really belong.

This academic view of the *development* of English prose, however, has its weaknesses. It is too ready to envisage the movement of English prose in the direction of the newspaper and the advertisement as an *advance*. Sometimes Tudor prose is treated patronizingly, as something worthy but crude and 'uncivilized', praised for its resources of narrative or invective, but condemned as 'inadequate' for argument, or dialectic, or philosophy, and above all for 'science'.

It can be argued though that the limitations of Tudor prose have been exaggerated. Richard Hooker (1554–1600) in his *Laws of Ecclesiastical Polity* provided a model of prose that was luminous, harmonious, and perfectly adapted to ratiocination and philosophical argument. And Swift said of the Bible: 'I doubt whether the alterations since introduced have added much to the beauty, or strength of the English tongue, though they have taken off a great deal from that simplicity which is one of the greatest perfections in any language.'

Prose styles, like mechanical inventions, depend on all kinds of social and economic factors if they are to become operative. Various spinning devices were apparently invented during the Elizabethan period, but the economic organization of Elizabethan England had no use for them. In the same way there was no necessity for the prose of polite intercourse or scientific analysis. It was not that the Elizabethan prose writers were *incapable* of writing simple, analytical prose—as we have seen some of them did: but, generally speaking, there was no call upon them to do so and they were more interested in exploring other aspects of human experience.

Their prose may not have been 'useful' for the scientist. But as a medium of muscular and emotional expression it had many advantages over the 'abstract' prose of modern times. Tudor society was in many ways still 'primitive', and Tudor prose still fulfilled some of the more primitive functions of language. It appealed not only to the eye that measures and the hand that weighs, but to the *whole* man. Its muscular content is in fact a large part of its 'meaning'. The relationship between word and thing, word and sensation, word and action, was far more intimate than it is to-day. It was 'the language really used by men' in the full sense of the term, for not only was it alive with the idiom of the market-place and the countryside, but it communicated, not the pale reflection of men's thoughts and feelings, but their very texture.

It is time that the prose writers of the age of newspaper headlines and advertisement hoardings began to explore again the resources of English prose that the Tudor writers understood so well. That would indeed be a 'Development'.

WORKING MEN'S COLLEGE LIBRARY

K

XI

PAINTING AND SCULPTURE

DAVID PIPER

AT the end of the fifteenth century European art had reached a most spectacular climax. The greatest artists then at work—such as Raphael, da Vinci, Michelangelo, Dürer—were not alone; the names of many of their contemporaries stand second only to theirs, and will be found in any history of European art; only the names of Englishmen do not appear.

It has never been fully explained why native English art did not respond fully to the ideals of the Renaissance; in the twelfth century English artists had had great influence on the Continent, and later they were again to win international fame. But in the sixteenth century, and indeed the seventeenth, England had no painters recognized in Europe as being of the first rank, with one possible exception, and he was a miniaturist. True, her sculptors were known on the Continent, but their names have not lived, and only in this century has scientific research suggested that a revaluation of their work is overdue. Generally, the up-to-date artists working in England were foreigners, and mostly second-rate: the

146

exception amongst these was Hans Holbein the Younger.

Factors contributing to this refusal to develop along European lines are fairly obvious, though they do not explain why Englishmen so reacted to difficulties—such as the dislocation of normal life by civil wars and by plagues—that were common to most countries. A more important setback was provided by Henry VIII—the adoption of Protestantism coupled with the dissolution of the monasteries. Henry VIII not only removed thus the richest and most constant patron of the arts, the Catholic Church, but he began the actual destruction of the English heritage of art. Up till then, the Church had commissioned artists liberally; but with the Reformation, the Puritans' horror of so-called 'idolatrous images' put a stop to this, and, all over the country, religious pictures, statues, and windows were broken with fanatic enthusiasm. The delight in destruction flagged after a while, but revived under Cromwell in the next century, and the damage is incalculable.

Thus the Church no longer provided a market on which the artist could depend for his living; landscape as an art in itself was not yet known; what remained then for the painter? First, there was his old stand-by, decorative painting: house-painting, far more elaborate than now, but limited to the houses of the rich. This included, however, the important branch of sign-painting; for not only inns, but shops and many private houses displayed signs. Secondly, there were decorations for pageants: these were numerous, and probably paid well; but as the decorations were scrapped as soon as the pageant was over, we have few records of them. Then there was portraiture. The demand for portraits, constant for centuries, depends on one of the most constant qualities of man—his vanity.

Vanity was not lacking in either Henry VIII's subjects,
or in Elizabeth's. But Henry VIII had destroyed another
patron besides the Church: the old aristocracy. In its
place he promoted a new class: men of tremendous wealth
and power, newly rich, and with an unbridled love of
display but a somewhat oppressive lack of taste: Wolsey
was typical of them. In Elizabeth's reign, taste was
refined: in literature, taste indeed became ultra-refined
and fashion demanded above all the curious and bizarre;
but although the age produced, besides the *Euphues* of
Lyly, the plays of Shakespeare, no genius was born to
interpret the Elizabethan spirit in paint. Thus the Elizabethan portrait tends to be over-stocked with display and
gorgeous detail: jewels, brocades, mottoes, allegorical
allusions, coats of arms, even sonnets—anything to
emphasize the importance and wealth of the sitter, down
to the new-fangled watches.

Sculptors were perhaps less badly hit by the Reformation, for though they lost their work in the churches,
they found it again in the great country houses going
up all over England: in the carving of stone doorways
and elaborate fireplaces, and above all in the making of
tombs. Tombs satisfied the same vanity as portraits:
often commissioned years before the death of those who
were to lie beneath them, they generally indeed were
portraits: the full-length effigy of man and wife, many
surrounded by the kneeling figures of their families.

The average London artist was a craftsman-tradesman.
If a painter, he would be a member of the Painter-
Stainers company, which tried ineffectually to keep a
monopoly of painting in the capital, and whose members
painted anything to order, from wagons to portraits. If
you were to call one of them an 'artist', he would not

have understood: the idea of the artist as a genius—courted by kings, wealthy and proud as a lord, with a code of morals and behaviour all of his own, yet admitted by the general public—was unknown to them. The seed of this idea of 'genius' could already be seen in the dominating personalities of certain Italian artists, but it was not fully popularized till the nineteenth century. Meanwhile the English painters worked anonymously and modestly as good tradesmen in their craft, producing the article demanded, portrait or wagon; many of their names are known from the records, and many of the pictures they must have painted still exist—but they worked in such an orthodox workshop style that one can scarcely be distinguished from another.

The foreigners working in England were mostly refugees, directly or indirectly, of religious persecution on the Continent, particularly the Low Countries. The greatest of them is almost the first: Hans Holbein the Younger (1497–1543). A German-Swiss from Basel, he came to England first in 1526, bearing a letter of introduction from his friend Erasmus, the great humanist scholar, to Sir Thomas More. For two years he worked for the latter in Chelsea, and for his friends. In 1528 he returned to Switzerland, but was back in England in 1532, to stay—apart from some brief journeys abroad—till he died, victim of the plague, in 1543.

During his first stay he does not seem to have been recognized much outside the circle of More's friends: at the beginning of his second stay (More being already in royal disfavour) he had indeed to fall back on foreign patrons, the rich Germanic merchants of the Steelyard in London. Only in 1536 did he win established position as a court-painter to Henry VIII.

Holbein was no revolutionary, rather a craftsman of genius. He knew what his patrons wanted, and gave it to them. His astounding skill and the lifelikeness of the result, in full-size portraits or in miniatures, was probably the immediate cause of his success; a good likeness, before the invention of photography, was essential. He caused as little trouble as possible, by doing the actual painting from quick chalk drawings done from the life: there were no tedious long sittings. Finally, he recognized his sitters' importance. This he managed to convey in a way that cannot be included under the heading of craftsmanship. All his portraits have superb poise and dignity, and yet, after looking at a series of them one has not the impression that he flattered his subjects. Thus, though he has left a composite portrait of the court of Henry VIII which has an unparalleled historical interest, his portraits of people whose names are now forgotten have no less interest. This can be said of very few court-painters.

Though Holbein must have had assistants at the end of his life, there was no one of sufficient strength to carry on his work, much less develop it. Apart from adopting various superficial tricks made fashionable by him, English painters continued as before, working with considerable feeling for line and little for colour, in a curious wooden way reminiscent of inn sign-board effigies. More flashy work was done by various Flemings, particularly Antonio Mor (1512–1576). Mor was in England for a very brief visit when Philip II of Spain came to marry Mary Tudor, whose portrait Mor painted. More typical and best-known of the Flemish artists was Hans Eworth (active about 1545–1573): yet he is perhaps best known only because he had a habit of signing his work, which enables modern critics at least to recognize his work without embarrassment. In merit he stands but little above some of his contemporaries, who apparently did not sign their works, and are therefore less easy to separate one from another. They all show superficial influence of Holbein—they borrow his poses—but none have his mastery; more Italian influence is visible in the treatment of colour, and of light and shade, but it was merely the stock-in-trade of the contemporary Flemish school.

Various Italian sculptors had been used by Henry VIII and by Wolsey—in particular Pietro Torrigiani (1472–1522), responsible for the tomb of Henry VII in Westminster Abbey—but the English masons also were conservative, and apart from borrowing again certain tricks from the Italians, continued in their own way, developing the art of the great formal tomb to a degree never surpassed in its kind, even though critics tend to ignore it, as they ignore Elizabethan painting, because they will not fit into the main stream of European art.

Indeed, towards the middle of Elizabeth's reign it is obvious that English conservatism has triumphed: the foreigners settled in England make their compromise with the stiff and linear native tradition. The result is the spectacular output of portraits which still hang in many old country houses. At the beginning of the century the whole-length portrait was unusual, but now it was exploited to enable the utmost magnificence of dress and jewels to be shown—the great wheel ruffs of men and women alike, the hooped skirts, the embroidered and padded doublets and trunks, and over all the pale mask of a face so conventional that almost any female portrait of this type may popularly be mistaken, and generally is, for that of Elizabeth herself.

The Queen had very pronounced ideas on painting, and it is perhaps owing to her influence that painting in England kept so firmly to its own line of development. Nicholas Hilliard (1547-1619), her appointed miniature painter, has described Elizabeth's sitting to him. She made him paint her 'in the goodly alley of a fair garden' so that no shadow should be on her face, and expressed her opinion that the modern Italian concern for light and shade arose from some shortcoming either in the painter or the sitter. Yet she was also critical of quality in English painting, and a draft for a proclamation exists, which states that, in view of the number of bad portraits of her in circulation, no one is to paint any more until 'some special cunning painter' had made an archetype or pattern from which all others might henceforth be copied. A number of bad portraits were in fact collected and destroyed at her order. She knew the value of portraits as propaganda for royal prestige, and the long series of paintings of her still in existence are at least supremely regal.

Hilliard is the gem of the age. Miniatures were the most fashionable form of painting: two or three inches high, they acted as photographs, and also as jewels that could be worn. They were exchanged by kings, by lovers, by parents and children, by husbands and wives. The fine linear treatment necessary in them had a great influence on the painting of life-size portraits, but what becomes a wooden stiffness and exaggerated attention to detail in the full-scale picture is redeemed in the miniature, especially in Hilliard's, by its very smallness. There is nothing mechanical in Hilliard, but a great liveliness and freshness, and his colour is startling. He was Holbein's true heir in England, and he acknowledges his debt:

'Holbein's manner of limning (miniature painting) I have ever imitated, and hold it for the best.' He was one of the first to be conscious of the dignity of his calling: 'I wish it were so that none should meddle with limning but gentlemen alone.'

All through the next century, the underlying conflict continues between the conservative English craft tradition and the more spectacular ideas and methods of the immigrant foreigners: Van Dyck, Lely, Kneller. The result was generally a compromise, though not always a happy one, until in the eighteenth century, Hogarth at once sums up the development of the two centuries before him, and provides a springboard for a new start, in which, at last, the native English artist predominates.

WORKING MEN'S COLLEGE
★ ★
LIBRARY

XII

ARCHITECTURE

ARTHUR OSWALD

THE historian, who in surveying the passage of time is accustomed to look before and after, might be tempted to describe the architecture of the sixteenth century in England as a period of faltering between two epochs. He might call it a debatable land, a frontier belt. Behind stand the mediæval mountains; just beyond the horizon lies the cultivated, ordered landscape of the classical age; the country between is indeterminate, not indeed lacking in features, which are sometimes surprising and even fantastic, but is essentially transitional in its character.

It is easy to stress too strongly the contrasts which Tudor architecture holds: the break-up of the Gothic system and the impact of Renaissance ideas, the abrupt cessation of church building and the transfer of interest to the aristocratic mansion. Throughout the century mediæval traditions persisted strongly, while the influence of the Renaissance showed itself only in features, tentatively and too obviously applied, in minutiæ of ornament and carving, and in a conscious effort to plan a house within a symmetrical frame. If the building of churches had gone on, as it did elsewhere in Europe, we should not be so acutely conscious of the cleft which seems to strike across the century. The less extravagant houses of the second half of Queen Elizabeth's reign are recognizably the children of those built when her father was on the throne. There is no great difference, for example, between Barrington Court and Montacute, two Somerset houses built, one during the early years of Henry VIII's reign, the other at the end of the century. Vernacular architecture was but little affected by the new ideas and developed mainly in satisfying the general demand for higher standards of comfort and convenience. The yeoman of 1600 normally had a fireplace with a chimney for himself to sit in and for his wife to cook at, whereas his grandparents had commonly known nothing better than an open hearth in a smoke-blackened hall.

When the sixteenth century dawned, there was not a sign to show that the last phase in the long history of Gothic architecture was drawing to a close. The feeling of security that prevailed, once Henry VII had firmly established his position on the throne, encouraged new building enterprises and the resumption of others interrupted or delayed during the Wars of the Roses. It is often maintained that there was a marked decrease in the volume of ecclesiastical building after 1500, and it is true that not many important works were carried out in the cathedrals and great monastic churches. But for the first quarter of the century activity was not less than during the thirty years before Bosworth, and it should be remembered that after four centuries of building few of the great churches were in need of further attention. Yet, between 1500 and the dissolution of the monasteries Bath Abbey was rebuilt, the canons of Ripon reconstructed their nave, Rochester acquired a new Lady chapel, Winchester a re-modelled presbytery, Peterborough its eastern termination, Christchurch Priory its choir vault. The detached bell-tower of Evesham Abbey was erected by the last abbot; at Fountains a great tower was added to the Cistercian abbey in disregard of the rules laid down by the founder of the order; and at Bolton a new west tower was begun, though never finished. The list is far from complete, and it ignores the many minor works, notably the chantry chapels, which continued to be built in large numbers, as well as the royal chapels, the crowning achievements of the age.

Numerous parish churches were enlarged or entirely rebuilt, sometimes by an individual benefactor but just as often by communal effort.* Many of the finest towers belong to this period. One need only mention Wrexham; All Saints, Derby; St. Mary, Beverley; St. Mary Magdalene, Taunton (rebuilt in the nineteenth century to the old design); Probus (Cornwall); Lavenham and Beccles (Suffolk); Wisbech (Cambs.); St. Neot's (Hunts.); Dedham (Essex); the upper stages of Boston 'Stump' and the spire of Louth. The building of towers was a source of local pride and rivalry, and, thanks to the popularity of change-ringing, was revived in the eighteenth century. An East Anglian testator, in forming a fund, or 'cofer', as he called it, for charitable purposes, directed that some of the

---

*For example, Lavenham and St. James, Bury St. Edmunds (Suffolk); Saffron Walden (Essex); St. Mary the Great, Cambridge; St. Andrew and St. Stephen, Norwich; St. Margaret, Westminster; Fairford and the nave of Cirencester (Glos.); Manchester (much enlarged); St. Michael le Belfry, York, by John Forman, master mason at York Minster. In some instances the work began during the last decade of the fifteenth century.

money should be spent 'in makyng of steples whereas the poure parish is not in powre to do yt'. A church without a steeple was something to be ashamed of. The date of this will is a little earlier than our period (1483), but the making of steeples went on right up to the Reformation, and some parishes, like Beccles, took advantage of the enforced sale of church ornaments in Edward VI's reign to complete their towers with the proceeds. The dissolution of the religious gilds and the confiscation of their possessions as well as the bewildering changes in the liturgy effectively discouraged any further building of church towers, or churches, after 1550.* The completion of the tower of Great St. Mary's Church, Cambridge, at the end of Queen Elizabeth's reign is an almost solitary instance.

The free use of such adjectives as 'decadent' and 'debased', which the Victorians applied to the last phase of our mediæval architecture, has cast a slur on Tudor Gothic which still lingers, in spite of the revaluation that has taken place in recent years. Time and again English artists have excelled in linear design, and in evolving what is conveniently termed Perpendicular architecture, and can more accurately be described as a rectilinear style, the master masons of the second half of the fourteenth century found a form of architectural expression peculiarly suited to the national temperament. It remained the basis of design for over two hundred years; and at Oxford, and in out-of-the-way parts of the country, where masons' traditions died slowly, it lived on until the beginning of the eighteenth century. Far from being

*At East Bergholt in Suffolk the building of the west tower never went beyond the first stage, and the bells still remain in the temporary timber cage set up in the churchyard to receive them.

exhausted in 1500, it was showing all the vigour of full maturity.

By this time the freemasons had acquired a technical mastery over their materials never previously attained, and in the fan vault a method of roofing in stone exact, economical, scientific and capable of the most exciting effects. Bath Abbey, the vaults of St. George's, Windsor, above all Henry VII's Chapel, for which a place would have to be found in any list of seven wonders of the Gothic world, were all works of the royal architects, the brothers Robert and William Vertue.* Another great architect of the period was John Wastell, responsible for the Bell Harry tower of Canterbury Cathedral, the completion of King's College Chapel, Cambridge, including the fan vault, and, on stylistic grounds, the eastern chapels at Peterborough. All three are among the finest achievements of the Perpendicular age. While the royal master masons, in works where money was not stinted, evolved new delicacies and intricacies of detail and dramatic effects that seem to cry out for applause, Wastell knew the value of plain wall surfaces for enhancing the effect of rich ornament or delicate mouldings, although at King's he was obliged to satisfy the royal penchant for heraldic display. How varied the achievement of the period was can be shown by adducing in contrast the grand and simple forms used in the tower of Lavenham or the nave of Ripon, the latter the work of Christopher Scune, the master mason who supervised the erection of the spire at Louth. There are instances, it is true, of coarse and skimped work, but these can be found in almost every age.

*Robert Vertue died in 1506, William in 1526. Associated with William Vertue in his later years was Henry Redman (died 1528).

The cessation of church building and adornment brought about by the dissolution of the monasteries and the introduction of the reformed liturgy left the field to secular architecture after Henry VIII's death. It had already been competing for pride of place as the royal palaces multiplied and prelates and courtiers rehoused themselves on a scale of splendour that sometimes resulted in their seats becoming royal palaces too. Such was the fate of Wolsey's York Place (re-christened Whitehall) and Hampton Court, both of which Henry VIII completed; and towards the end of his reign he compelled Archbishop Cranmer to give up Otford and Knole. Characteristic of the houses built by courtiers at the time are Hengrave Hall, Suffolk, and Sutton Place, near Guildford, the latter decorated with Renaissance detail in terracotta, which is also to be seen at Layer Marney in Essex. After the dissolution those newly enriched by the spoils of the monasteries proceeded to build houses for themselves on the sites, usually converting the domestic buildings ranged round the cloister, but sometimes utilizing part of the church itself, as did Wriothesley at Titchfield, where he built his house, now in its turn a ruin, within the nave of the Priory. Queen Elizabeth's economical nature did not allow her to indulge in much building; she was more interested in disposing of some of the palaces inherited from her father; but she expected her ministers and favourites to house her and her retinue handsomely when she visited them. Both Lord Burghley and Sir Christopher Hatton acknowledged that the main reason for the extravagance into which they were led was to do honour to the Queen.

Nearly all the Early Tudor palaces and country houses conformed to the closed courtyard plan of the previous century, with the great hall normally, though not invariably, placed opposite the gatehouse. Brick was extensively used, being not only cheaper than stone outside the stone regions, but more rapidly produced and laid—an asset when the King's impatience could only be satisfied if building was pushed on by night as well as by day. Skylines were enlivened by ornamented chimney-stacks arranged in striking groups, often octagonal in shape or twisted, by heraldic finials and by turret tops of ogee form. Windows are almost always square-headed and have been simplified by omitting the cusps from the lights. The turreted and battlemented gatehouse survived as a symbol from the feudal age. It is a conspicuous feature of the Oxford and Cambridge college buildings of the period, which in design and plan are closely related to the country house. Christ's and St. John's at Cambridge, Corpus Christi at Oxford, built during the first two decades of the century, show the typical quadrangular arrangements. Wolsey's Oxford college, which became Christ Church, was a more ambitious project, but languished after his fall, although re-established as a royal foundation. Trinity College, Cambridge, was a dying gesture of the King. It took sixty years to reduce to a quadrangular shape the buildings of the pre-existing colleges which were incorporated in the new foundation, but the Great Court, as it finally emerged, is an epitome of Tudor architecture, with its great gateway, chapel, hall and ranges of chambers, all mediæval in spirit, enclosing a courtyard the centre of which is occupied by a Renaissance fountain.*

Up to 1550 Renaissance influence on our architecture

*The hall and fountain belong to the first decade of the seventeenth century.

WORKING MEN'S
COLLEGE
LIBRARY

Country Life

BARRINGTON COURT

is hardly discernible, in spite of the numerous foreign artists and sculptors introduced by Henry VIII. By commissioning Torrigiano to design the tomb of his father and by patronizing other Italians, notably Benedetto da Rovezzano and Giovanni da Maiano, he went direct to the fountain-head of Renaissance art, but it is only in sculpture and wood-carving that the new forms are to be seen. Cherubs and arabesques are found on tombs and screens, replacing angels and the vine-trail; pilasters begin to make an appearance. The superb woodwork of King's College Chapel, Cambridge, is wholly Renaissance in character, but this is without doubt by foreign carvers, though they have not yet been identified. At Hampton Court there are the terracotta busts of emperors in roundels built into the walls and the Italianate pendants to the hall roof. Nonsuch, the last of Henry VIII's palaces and the most extravagant, was less a work of architecture than of plasterwork; its timber-framed structure was covered with plaster statues and reliefs of classical subjects. These drew the admiration of Evelyn, the diarist, who saw the building a few years before it was pulled down: 'a Gothic fabric', he noted, 'but these walls incomparably beautified'.

After the breach with Rome direct contact with Italy almost ceased and the second wave of Renaissance ideas came by way of the Low Countries. For the next seventy years, until Inigo Jones returned from his visit to Italy, classic architecture was known in England chiefly through the strange distorting mirrors of Flemish, Dutch and German designers. There was also a slight infusion of French influence. The fantastic strapwork ornament, the foreigners' pattern books, were copied by joiners, carvers and masons, and soon ousted the old Gothic forms of

L

decoration or were combined with them in a curious and sometimes not unattractive *mélange*. The exuberance of the new ornament appealed to the Elizabethans. Delicacy or refinement would not have been appreciated by a generation of *parvenus* if either had been offered them; but designers and patrons alike delighted in the novelties purveyed and in the new world of ideas that they seemed to have opened. Elizabethan taste was much like that of the Victorians in its indiscriminate love of opulence for its own sake; there had to be much to show for money spent, and foreign fashions were at a premium.

Sir Thomas Gresham's Royal Exchange, built in 1566–1567 and destroyed in the Great Fire of London, was the most important Renaissance building erected in England during Queen Elizabeth's reign. It was the work of a Flemish architect, Master Henryk, who also found a patron in Lord Burghley. Its most notable feature was its Renaissance cloister forming the ground storey enclosing the courtyard. Hollar's engraving shows a building that is an obvious exotic, imported from the Netherlands, but claiming architectural distinction as well as novelty. At Cambridge Doctor Caius employed Theodore Haveus, an architect from Cleves, to design an elaborate sundial for his college and perhaps also the classic ornaments of his three symbolic gateways, but the little Gate of Honour, with its miniature temple façades, is a work of sculpture rather than architecture. As in the earlier Italianate phase, sculptors and wood carvers set the fashion, and the progress of Renaissance ideas is best studied in the church monuments, many of which were designed by foreigners who had set up shop in England.

But gradually and with hesitation the new forms came to be applied to architecture, often looking like grafts on an old stock. In 1563 was published the first English architectural book, John Shute's *Chief Groundes of Architecture,* in which the orders were figured. Soon most English masons could design something that would pass muster for a classic doorway with a semicircular arch and a pair of columns or pilasters; mouldings began to assume classic profiles; gables burgeoned with classic finials. In the interiors chimneypieces and ceilings displayed a medley of ill-digested Renaissance motives, and the massive furniture—four-posters, court cupboards, chests and buffets—was designed to accord. Crude and coarse as much of the work is, it has a vigour and spontaneity that the products of more refined ages lack. The wood-worker was often in advance of the mason, but, while many exteriors remained sober and unaffected, great houses such as Longleat, Burghley House, Kirby Hall and Wollaton show the new features applied to their elevations and skylines. Occasionally, as at Lacock Abbey and Kirby Hall, even the chimneys are classicized and become columns bearing an entablature.

The plan of country houses underwent an important change. Even where the courtyard was retained there was a striving after symmetry, which had either eluded or failed to worry an earlier generation. But in the majority of houses the courtyard was abandoned for a plan comprising a main range with balancing wings and frequently taking the form of an E or H. The entrance was placed centrally in all the larger houses, and the hall was disposed in such a way that you entered through the screens passage at the lower end in the time-honoured fashion. It often needed ingenuity to make this possible, but Elizabethan planning excelled in solving problems posed by the interests of symmetry. The great hall with open timber roof continued to be built, notably in the Oxford and Cambridge colleges and the inns of court, but also in some of the most up-to-date mansions. In the majority of instances, however, the hall was now restricted to one storey and given a flat ceiling. Its importance as the focus of the life of the household was diminishing as the owner and his family acquired new standards of comfort and segregated themselves more and more from their retainers and servants. But the hall had still a long process of minimizing to go through before becoming a mere vestibule.

The E or H plan was well adapted to a clear-cut division between the private apartments and the offices and servants' quarters, placed in opposing wings. Off the upper end of the hall opened the withdrawing room or parlour, and a separate 'eating room' was provided for the family. Other rooms included the great chamber, a study, and sometimes a winter parlour; and nearly all the larger houses had a long gallery for indoor exercise, dancing and music. The gallery was sometimes placed in the middle or top storey of the private wing, or, alternatively, might run the full length of the main range, as at Montacute. The spiral stair of the mediæval house gave way to broader ascents, going up in short flights with landings between, often accommodated in square projections set in the angles where main range and wings joined. Elizabethan houses are frequently sited with their principal front facing north on account of the prevalent belief that the south wind brought with it noxious vapours. Ranges continued to be built only one room thick with lighting from both sides.

John Thorpe's drawings show clearly how intensely interested in planning were the Elizabethan designers

and how ingeniously they arranged their rooms to preserve the symmetry of their elevations.* Thorpe was a
surveyor rather than an architect and his long career over-
lapped into the following century, but on his plan of
Kirby Hall he noted that he laid the first stone in
1570. His studies are chiefly of building by other architects—Wollaton, for example, was the work of Robert
Smithson. He was acquainted with Vredeman de Vrie's
book of architecture and made studies from Du Corceau,
but the type of detail which appears in his drawings is
more often Dutch than French. Yet stripped of their
ornament, the elevations remain characteristically
English.

The rectilinear basis of design is as obvious in
Thorpe's drawings as in the buildings of the time. The
jutting bays and turrets accented the perpendicular lines
of the elevations and these were countered by the hori-
zontal bands of plinth, string courses and parapet. In the
windows of early Tudor buildings there were arched
heads to the lights; these were eliminated in the second
half of the century, so that the window became a rectilinear pattern of intersecting mullions and transoms. The
skylines were enlivened by gables, fancifully shaped or
straight-sided, as well as by the prominent chimney-stacks
and the little cupolas of ogee form crowning turrets

*The Thorpe collection of drawings is in Sir John Soane's
Museum, Lincolns Inn Fields. Mr. John Summerson's recently
published paper, 'John Thorpe and the Thorpes of Kingscliffe'
(*The Architectural Review*, Nov. 1949), has set Thorpe's career
in a new light. He was by profession a land-surveyor, but he came
of a family of Northamptonshire masons and was obviously
keenly interested in contemporary architecture. Designing for
him can have been only a spare-time occupation and perhaps did
not amount to more than supplying sketch plans and 'uprights'
(i.e. elevations for lesser Court officials).

which remained fashionable all through the century. In some of the later buildings, however, we find a reaction in favour of a flat skyline, with a pierced parapet, against which the chimneys and turrets stand out with greater effect; and several of the best-known houses of the next reign, Hatfield and Audley End, for example, dispense with gables. In the exterior of Hardwick Hall, 'more window than wall', Elizabethan architecture is seen in undisguised form without the foreign trappings. Apart from the strapwork flourishes on the towers it is a design of verticals and horizontals in sharp opposition but with the vertical lines predominating. With the arch discarded because no longer necessary, this is the Perpendicular style carried to its logical conclusion.

The native English tradition is best seen in the less pretentious buildings, the numerous manor houses of the stone regions and the brick halls of East Anglia. By ringing the changes on three, four, five or seven gables, with projecting porch and bay windows, great variety was obtained in the elevations without resort to Renaissance ornament. Moyns Park (Essex), Chequers (Bucks.) in brick; Mells Manor (Somerset), Cold Ashton (Glos.), Wroxton Abbey (Oxfordshire), Fountains Hall (York-shire), in stone: these are half a dozen examples, chosen almost at random, for the list could be extended in-definitely. The timber-framed 'magpie' houses of the north-west illustrate even more clearly the continuance of mediæval methods of design and construction.

In addition, there are the humbler dwellings of yeoman families, and the market houses, grammar schools and almshouses, although the best examples of the three last categories belong chiefly to the following century. The farmer class participated in the building rush with the same eagerness as their superiors, if not by reconstructing from the foundations, at least by inserting chimneys into their hall houses and cutting up the hall with a floor across its upper half. In the second part of *Henry VI* Shakespeare makes one of Jack Cade's Kentish followers say of their leader:

> Sir, he made a chimney in my father's house, and the bricks are alive at this day to testify it.

Shakespeare referred to a process that was taking place all over the Weald in his day with the growing cheapness and availability of brick. In wealthy East Anglia the clothiers and sheep farmers seem to have been able to afford chimneys of bricks and mortar at an earlier date, and many richly-carved fireplaces of Henry VII's and Henry VIII's reigns are found in their houses.

The dividing line of the century cuts arbitrarily across the sequence of architectural development. The houses of James I's reign show much the same characteristics as those built between 1580 and 1600, though the emphasis on classic features, still borrowed from the Low Countries, becomes more marked. It remained for Inigo Jones to introduce pure Italian models into England and for his disciples and successors to complete the long-drawn-out process which at last gave us classic architecture.

WORKING MEN'S COLLEGE LIBRARY

XIII

MUSIC

RALPH HILL

"The English could lay claim to be the best-looking,
the most musical and to the best tables of any people."
—*Erasmus.*

An historical period such as the Middle Ages or the Victorian Era is as temporarily inaccurate as any such generalization must be. The Middle Ages, for example, were not something that can be accurately measured in time, something that has a beginning and an end, like the 9.15 p.m. from King's Cross to Edinburgh or a performance of *Hamlet*. Indeed the beginning and the end of the Middle Ages are deeply rooted in the past and in the future, and any line of demarcation can be drawn only in an arbitrary manner.

In speaking of the Tudor Period as it affects the Tudor Kings and Queens and their actions it is correct to say that it began in the year 1485 and ended in 1603. But directly we begin to apply those dates to describe a style of art, a system of economy, or a religious ideal the lines of demarcation, 1485 and 1603, possess neither meaning nor truth: the tree has been dismembered and has become a mere trunk without roots or branches. In terms of music, the distinctive style and character of the Tudor Period evolved slowly and imperceptibly from the music of previous generations and equally slowly and imperceptibly dissipated itself during the first half of the seventeenth century.

Unfortunately, the dissipation led to the end of a great period and not to something new and vital, as it did in Italy and Germany. Mainly because of the Civil War, the

rise of Puritanism, and finally the 'spiritually catastrophic infliction upon this country of a string of petty German princelets, the preposterous Hanoverian Georges, and all that they stood for in the way of boorishness, Bœotian uncultivation, provincial ignorance, bourgeois narrowness, and bestial stupidity', English music was finally stifled by German and Italian influences which remained supreme, outside the lighter styles of music, from the end of the seventeenth century to the beginning of the twentieth century.

169

In the fourteenth and fifteenth centuries the establishing of the printing press and of an effective system of musical notation led to a universal dissemination and appreciation of music. The development and mastery of the contrapuntal style of writing and the growth of secular music offered new and fascinating resources to the composer. He exploited these resources for the delectation of that amateur and professional musical public, which grew larger and larger as a new middle class society came into being during the growth of the Reformation in the first half of the sixteenth century.

This society was largely represented by the merchant class, which became larger and more wealthy as English overseas trade expanded. It was inevitable that these merchants should want to emulate the aristocracy and to challenge its mode of living, in fact there was a considerable amount of intermarriage between the two classes, and the tendency was to leave the town and set up home in the country, building comfortable and compact manor houses and converting those mediæval castles and manor houses best suited to modern requirements.

This resulted in the encouragement and enjoyment of leisure and luxury in quiet and secluded surroundings. Thus the arts of music, painting, and poetry received keen and ready patronage among the members of this new society. Indeed, the famous amateur musician Roger North, writing in the eighteenth century, mentions certain families 'whose ancestors made the musicall enterteinement a family provision for spending the superfluous time'.

The centre of musical activity was no longer the Church but the Court. Henry VII did much to encourage instrumental music and was a composer himself. So was

Henry VIII, who favoured light, simple, and merry dance music—the jig, hornpipe, galliard, pavane, and the domp. Both at Court and in the country manor houses the favourite domestic instruments were the regals (a portable organ), the virginal (a keyboard instrument similar to the spinet and harpsichord), the lute, and the chest or cupboard of viols which consisted of five or six instruments corresponding to-day to the violin family. The viols would be played not only by members of the family, but by paid professional musicians.

By the second half of the sixteenth century chamber music became established as an indepedent branch of the art of music with it own distinctive style. Few students of musical history realize that chamber music received its first impetus in England and not in Germany as commonly supposed. However, to use the words of Professor J. A. Westrup, 'it was through the concerted vocal forms that composers had learned to handle easily and convincingly the stubborn art of polyphony. For centuries the main functions of instruments had been to support voices or to join in concert with them. That easy-going exchange which enabled an instrument to supply the place of a missing voice also made it possible to supply all the voices by instruments; but it did not at first lead to any marked difference of style, even when at the Renaissance music came to be written for instruments only. As lute accompaniments to a solo voice tended to preserve, if only by suggestion, the lineaments of polyphonic writing, so pieces for string instruments were modelled, in the early stages, on motets or madrigals for voices. This meant the transference of phrases originally conceived for singing, the adoption of the original practice of entries at different levels, and the avoidance of extremes of compass.

171

Familiarity with the new medium led naturally to the growth of a style more characteristic of instruments, and this was encouraged by the high standard already achieved in the manufacture of string instruments in the sixteenth century.'

The most important instrumental form was the Fancy, which was the English equivalent of the Italian Fantasia that, like the Madrigal, was introduced by Italian musicians employed at the Tudor court. The Fancy, which became very complex in style and texture, was aptly described by Thomas Morley in his *Plaine and Easie Introduction to Practicall Musicke* (1597). This music 'without a dittie', is made 'when a musician taketh a point at his pleasure, and wresteth and turneth it as he list, making either much or little of it according as shall seeme best in his own conceit'. This clearly suggests the free and contrapuntal characteristics of the music. Less complex and more adaptable to amateurs was the instrumental music based on the popular dance forms of the period, which Henry VIII favoured so highly.

Much fine music was also written for keyboard instruments—the virginals (which was the favourite instrument of Queen Elizabeth who played well), the spinet, and the harpsichord. Among the outstanding published collections of keyboard pieces were *Parthenia, My Ladye-Nevell's Booke* (which included forty-two pieces by William Byrd) and *Fitzwilliam Virginal Book,* which contains three hundred pieces by John Bull, William Byrd, Thomas Morley, Thomas Tallis, Dowland, and others.

The Tudor period is often described as the 'Golden Age of English Music'; this, of course, refers essentially to vocal music, both liturgical and secular, rather than instrumental music, which was only in its infancy. Vocal polyphony reached its zenith of ingenuity and expressiveness in England. In quality and number the English school of composers, at least during the sixteenth century, surpassed all foreign competitors, and from early Tudor times there flourished literally hundreds of good composers. Most of their names are now forgotten and their works remain unpublished. Out of the half-dozen greatest names in Europe at least two are English: the French Josquin des Près (1445–1521), the Italian Palestrina (1526–1594), the Spanish Vittoria (1540–1613), the Belgian Orlando de Lassus (1530–1594), and the English William Byrd (1542–1623) and Thomas Tallis (1515–1585). It is interesting to note that the eminent American musicologist, Paul Henry Láng, says that 'after Shakespeare, Byrd is without doubt the most imposing figure of the English Renaissance, towering above all his contemporaries. When discussing him, comparisons can be made only to the other "princes" of music, Palestrina and Lassus, and, indeed, he has been called the English Palestrina'.

On January 22, 1575, Queen Elizabeth granted a licence jointly to William Byrd and Thomas Tallis 'Gentl' of our Chapell' giving them a monopoly of printing and setting music and music paper. It was also forbidden 'to bring or cause to be brought out of any forren Realmes into any of our dominions any songe or songes made and printed in any forren countrie upon paine of our high displeasure'. The licence covered a period of twenty-one years, and it was during this time that great innovations took place in the production of English printed music.

We know little more about Byrd than we do about

Shakespeare. So far as can be ascertained from existing records, he was a very careful and stable man, but he possessed a strong will and a natural pugnacity which displayed itself in the tenacious management of his general affairs. He was what we like to imagine is the typical Englishman. His versatility was extraordinary. He excelled in church music, in madrigals, and in instrumental music, notably for the virginals and for various combinations of strings. Apart from the lyrical beauty and expressiveness of his music, as a contrapuntist his ingenuity is fit to be placed alongside that of the greatest masters of vocal polyphony of all time.

One of the glories of the Golden Age was the Madrigal, which like the Motet and the Fancy originated in Italy. However, madrigal writing in England reached a higher stage of development in quantity, variety, ingenuity, and expressiveness than perhaps in any other country. It is said that over ninety-two collections of madrigals were published in England during the years 1588–1638. 'Madrigals were much in use in the reign of Queen Elizabeth,' says a foreign resident, 'in which compositions the English of that time had left proof of their ability even to vie with the best Italian composers. Nobody could then pretend to a liberal education, who had not made such progress in music as to be able to sing his part at sight and it was usual when ladies and gentlemen met, for madrigal books to be laid before them, and everyone to sing their part . . . but since the glorious reign of Queen Elizabeth, music (for which, as well as her sister arts, England was then renowned all the world over) has been neglected as much by the little encouragement it has received from the great, as by reason of the civil war, that at length this art was entirely lost.'

The Elizabethan song-books, from which the ladies and gentlemen would sing their parts at sight, were of two distinct kinds—the madrigal and the lute-song. The madrigal is an unaccompanied song scored usually for no fewer than three voices and no more than six, each part being of equal impulse and interest. It is constructed out of short musical phrases, which are developed contrapuntally. The Rev. E. H. Fellowes, our leading expert on English madrigals, says that 'the true madrigal was seldom set to more than one stanza of poetry; and indeed these composers studied their words so closely, and expressed themselves with such intimate regard for the particular meaning of each word and each phrase, that the exact repetition of their music to a fresh stanza of words was scarcely ever possible. Every kind of device was employed by the composers both to secure variety and to sustain interest; and above all other considerations, they strove to add meaning and point to the words they had chosen to set.'

The madrigalists knew how to be grave as well as gay. They were inspired by moral, religious, and even mundane subjects; they extolled the virtues of the Morris Dance and the May-Day revels; they could express the feelings of passionate emotion as well as the light-hearted conceits of the nymphs and shepherds. Indeed, emotional expression and word-painting became the *raison d'être* of the madrigal as well as other vocal forms. An elaborate and subtle system of musical symbolism prevailed, and as certain of the older technical devices became outworn new ones were introduced to give fresh impetus to the emotional and pictorial possibilities of musical expression.

The music of the madrigals was printed in separate

part-books, one for each voice. There were no bar lines to break the free flow of the rhythm and phrasing, which the words and the melodic line demanded.

The Lute-Song, sometimes called an Ayre, is a solo song with several stanzas of words, for each of which the music is repeated, with a lute accompaniment supported by a bass viol to give it an added weight. The accompaniment being choral or harmonic rather than contrapuntal. Alternatively the vocal lines were harmonized for three voices so that the song could be sung by a quartet of voices. The English Ayre of which John Dowland was the greatest exponent during the short period of 1597 to 1622, looks forward to the new age of harmony.

Any study of the vocal music of the Tudor period necessarily involves the study of contemporary poetry, for the two arts continued to be interdependent up to the seventeenth century when they eventually parted company and went their own distinctive ways.

The names of the authors of the words set in the Elizabethan song-books were never given, despite the fact that there were among them some of the greatest of Shakespeare's contemporaries. It may be said that most of these poems were worthy of the music and they represent the cream of the lyric poetry of the period. Both the music and the words of Elizabethan song expressed the prevailing spirit of joy and freedom, the 'reasonable joy in life of a people freed from mediæval and not yet oppressed by Puritan complexes and fears'.

WORKING MEN'S COLLEGE LIBRARY

WORKING MEN'S
COLLEGE
LIBRARY

Anͦ · DNI · 1571 ·
ÆTATIS · SVÆ
· 29 ·

Sir Richard Grenville, killed
in a sea-fight near the Azores.
1591

SIR RICHARD GRENVILLE
1571. By an unknown artist

XIV

VOYAGERS

J. E. MORPURGO

SUCCEEDING ages have sought new emancipation: religious or political liberty, industrial development, the use of steam, electric and atomic power, the conquest of the air and its present adventure into supersonic speed. The sixteenth century burst the stringent bounds of mediæval existence and drove out into uncharted seas and unexplored lands.

The motives of individual adventurers were not always worthy, but, whether for gold or for God, whether to practise piracy or to enslave the negro, whether the inspiration was inquisitive or acquisitive, whether the aim was personal glory or a patriotic inclination to tickle the power of Spain at its sensitive extremities; whatever the impulse, no historical moralizing can diminish the amazing achievement of an age that made a continent into a world.

Despite the chauvinistic paeans of contemporaries and the able supporting chorus of nineteenth-century historians, the achievement was not exclusively British. In fact, England, exhausted by cross-Channel struggles and

M

by civil war, came late into the field of exploration. Henry VII let pass the opportunity to sponsor Columbus; but made some amends with a royal patent to Giovanni Cabot (1450–1498) (known to Bristol and to British history as *John* Cabot), and to this Genoese by birth, Venetian by naturalization and man of Bristol by residence, Henry paid a reward of ten pounds for the discovery of Cape Breton Island; yet Henry VII's·principal contribution to the destiny of an island empire was indirect. In the words of Francis Bacon, 'he could not endure to see trade sick'. He transfused new life into the English mercantile marine; passed through his first Parliament an encouraging Navigation Act (reserving to English ships the considerable import of wines and dyes from France); and then, with true Tudor craftiness, shook the hand raised to destroy; protecting English trade from its most powerful rivals, Spain and the Netherlands, by concluding trade treaties with those countries.

His son continued his policy of fostering English nautical and mercantile endeavour, and, in the history of English exploration—as in the history of English religion, English literature, English painting and English music—Henry VIII must have creditable mention.

But, before England was strong enough to grope beyond European seas, other powers were at work around all the continents except Australasia. The French explored the rivers of Canada. The Portuguese, by the not-so-simple expedient of visiting and claiming for themselves new lands, extended their domains in Africa, and there, as in India and in Brazil, they combined exploitation, proselytizing, exploration and empire-building. The Italians went everywhere and, having no centralized power behind them to claim dominion over their discoveries, gained nothing. Cortes (1485–1547), with less than six hundred Europeans, two hundred and fifty Indians, fifteen horses and ten brass cannon, conquered Mexico for Spain, while other Spaniards, seeking riches and converts, established Spain in Florida, entered the Gulf of California, touched at the mouth of the Mississippi, and won the islands of the Caribbean and parts of Central and South America. The Dutch went east to the Indies, but among the names of the great sixteenth-century travellers, the Netherlands is best represented by four stay-at-home Dutchmen. By their practical improvements in the art of map-making, the cartographers Gerhard Kremer (usually known as Mercator) (1512–1594), Abraham Ortelius (1527–1598), the hydrographer Lucas Wagenaer (c. 1540) and the printer Christopher Plantin (1514–1589), relieved seamanship of the fantastic legends of the Middle Ages.

And the greatest explorer of them all was a German Pole, who once his student-days were over, seldom left Prussia: Nicholas Copernicus (1473–1543), whose astronomical studies convinced scholar and adventurer alike that the world is a revolving globe, and made navigation from an act of faith into a science.

England's slow start in exploration served but to tighten the springs of endeavour. National pride, national avarice, and the new diplomatic importance of England in the affairs of Europe demanded that England should not remain forever outside the exciting treasure-hunt. Henry VIII was not so absorbed in international and matrimonial intrigue that he had not the time to select the right men to lead the English enterprises. By showing especial favour to William Hawkins (d. 1553), who between 1530 and 1532 made three voyages to Brazil by way of the Guinea coast, Henry's royal smiles launched into adventure the family, that, more often than any other family, was to fly its flag at the head of British maritime effort throughout the century.

For the most part, however, English advenurousness was still limited and followed but tamely in the steps of the continentals. In the Mediterranean and on the nearer coasts of Africa, on fishing voyages to Iceland, and around our own shores, England trained her seamen while her merchants grew rich in peace, and merchants and seamen inspired each other to covetous dreams of Cathay and the Indies.

Imitation of other powers was obviously fruitless. England must slip competition and seek different routes by which to tap the wealth of the East. In the reign of Edward VI, while the youthful invalid was at his pious task of mending the educational mischief wrought by the dissolution of the monasteries, Sir Hugh Willoughby (d. 1554), with Richard Chancellor (d. 1556) as pilot-general, set out to seek new knowledge with which to plague the scholars of Edward's foundations, and new wealth to bolster the Court and the City of London. It was their intention to find a way to India through the Arctic—the North-East Passage. Willoughby died in Russian Lapland, but Chancellor sailed into the White Sea and made his way by land to Moscow; still far from India, but not far from riches. He got safely back to England, and having helped to initiate the prototype of the great trading companies—the Muscovy Company—went once more to Russia by the Northern Route. On the homeward voyage he was lost at sea, but his convoy brought in a very real proof of progress—the first Russian Ambassador to London.

His old colleague in the Levantine trade, Anthony Jenkinson (d. 1611), succeeded to Chancellor, and thrusting out from Chancellor's furthest exploration, reached the Caspian and went on to Persia. Nearer and nearer to the East, but not yet by a route that could be considered practicable!

The Marian interlude disrupted exploration. Mary herself was not so un-English as to wish inactivity upon her sailors, but her husband, Philip II, was too Spanish to permit English competition. Yet even this interpolation acted as a catalyst upon English ambitions. Calais was lost, and with it went the last continental vent for excess energy. The indignity of post-Spanish rule hastened the choice of the Spaniard as an Englishman's enemy by birthright; and Spaniards were best molested where Spanish power was at its weakest. Mary's Catholic zeal turned martyrology into a national hobby and made the horrors of the Inquisition more comprehensible to England's instinctively Protestant conscience. All this to such good effect that when Elizabeth lifted, once more, the national hem from the dusty path to Rome, privateering upon Spanish trade-routes and upon Spanish Imperial preserves became at once a patriotic pastime, a religious duty and a gainful employment.

It was not a new habit. Already in 1540 the *Barbara* of London had performed loyal deeds of piracy on the South American coasts. But Elizabeth's impudent diplomacy and her inherited gift for choosing the right men; for knighting the boldest marauders and enriching the rovers who brought her most riches; built a navy, made buccaneering respectable and set the sails of English adventurers, so that, in her reign, their efforts caught and outstripped the rest of Europe.

Privateering was now a trade for gentlemen, for commoners and even for poets (Thomas Lodge (1558?–1625) began his *Margarite of America* on a ship in the Straits of Magellan) and, with privateering, commercial enterprise, discovery and—once war with Spain had broken out—national defence, were inextricably bound up.

The career of the greatest of Elizabethan sea-captains, Sir Francis Drake (1542–1596), like the careers of most of his colleagues, was of a nature that defies the niceness of reference-book definition. Though he was associated with the trading schemes of the Hawkins family, he was himself more often freebooter than merchant. Without a Royal commission he nevertheless entered upon a treaty with the Sultan of Ternate that, for many years, was respected by mercantile opinion as the cornerstone of English trade-rights in Asia. Where there was no war *de jure* in which he could fight Elizabeth's battles, then Sir Francis Drake made war *de facto* on his own account. He harried the Spaniards wherever he found them: in their home ports, in the West Indies and off the coasts of South America, by sea when they could be attacked at sea, by land when necessary. On first seeing the Pacific, in 1572, the pirate turned devout visionary and 'besought Almighty God of His goodness to give him life and leave to sail once in an English ship in that sea'. God, apparently more obliging than the Queen, gave him his chance, but when, between December 1577 and September 1580, still without official status, Drake circumnavigated the globe, he was as eager for loot as for discovery and as quick to fight as to explore. On his return, the Queen, made uncomfortable by the vigorous and undoubtedly legitimate protests of the Spanish Ambassador, was forced to withhold her approval of the activities of the 'arch-pirate' until such time as she felt strong enough to proclaim openly her readiness for war with Spain. Not until 1585 did England's most successful sailor become an officer in the Queen's navy, and thereafter, though he played a considerable part in the defeat of the Armada, the exploits of the licensed Admiral never equalled, in daring or good fortune, the exploits of the unauthorised filibuster.

Drake deserves his shrine in English legend as the glory of Elizabethan adventure and the epitome of naval daring, but, to the eventual evolution of England's maritime power, his cousin, Sir John Hawkins (1532–1595), was probably more important. Hawkins' reputation has been tarnished in retrospect by his part in the inauguration of the slave-trade, but Hawkins was merchant, and, above all, organizer, as well as adventurer. He had no itch for plunder, and even his slaving voyages of 1562, 1564–65 and 1567 were designed primarily to bully Spain into granting trading concessions. His greatest successes were achieved where most Elizabethan sailors found only frustration, in Court political circles. In 1578 he was made Treasurer of the Navy, and in that office, in association with Burghley, he built up the navy, improved 'Admiralty' administration, and developed England's maritime muscles to meet the strength of Spain.

The dream of successful trade and fabulous riches in the East grew with the heightened reports of returning voyagers. In 1576 Sir Humphrey Gilbert (1539?–1583), by his *Discourse on a North-West Passage to India*, revived Willoughby's North-East Passage theory only to cast ridicule upon it. But in its place he put the suggestion that India could be reached by sailing in a North-Westerly direction. Not all the doubts cast by the voyages of Martin

Frobisher (1535–1594) to the inhospitable coasts of Labrador in 1576, 1577 and 1578, nor all the failures of other navigators, could dim the bright hopes.

Others, accepting the lure of the East with less visionary bias, were content to follow the conventional routes. In 1600 Captain William Adams (1564–1620) settled in Japan and was there received 'in such favour with two emperors as never was any Christian in those parts of the world'. In the same year, on the last day of the century, a charter was granted to the East India Company; the company that was to prove the most influential, and, next to the Hudson Bay Company, the longest-lived of all the great overseas trading companies. But the idea that a North-West Passage might be found persisted and tantalized English ambition for a generation.

And, in the fruitless search for the Passage, the most significant development of sixteenth-century mercantile policy took growth. Appreciating the fact that the Straits of Magellan, though still the golden gateway to plunder, were not the ideal route to Eastern trade, and frustrated in their hope of a North-West Passage, Gilbert himself, his half-brother, Sir Walter Raleigh (1552–1618), and their neighbour, Sir Richard Grenville (1542?–1591) saw worthy compromise on the East coast of America. This coast had been well reconnoitred by English privateers and by navigators searching for the opening of the North-West Passage. If it can ever be convenient to cross the Atlantic in a ship only just over one-thousandth of the size of the *Queen Elizabeth*, then the American coast could be called conveniently accessible. It was, too, comparatively unexploited by continental powers.

At first merchants and adventurers still looked beyond America to the East, thinking to establish trading-posts which, while making a little profit from barter with the American Indians, could act as revictualling stations for English ships on their way to more lucrative trade with the Indians of Asia. But gradually the eyes of England focused on America itself and prospects of colonization took the place of plans for temporary settlement. At home the geographers settled to the work of popularizing the new projects, and the writings of the greatest of these advertising agents of adventure, Richard Hakluyt (1552?–1616)—at once records of the past and incentives for the future—set America firm in English consciousness.

Gilbert's attempt to settle Newfoundland ended in disaster and in the death of its originator. Raleigh came nearer to success at Roanoke Island, but his colony disappeared into the mists of tragedy, and even the tobacco that he brought back, 'the vegetable of singular strength and power', was of no economic importance until John Rolfe invented a method of curing that made the plant sympathetic to European palates.

There was as yet no Empire. Only, in the next reign, after the establishment of Jamestown could a wise-after-the-event playwright (be he Shakespeare or Fletcher) put into the mouth of Cranmer his prophecy on the omni-presence of the English monarchy:

> *Wherever the bright sun of heaven shall shine*
> *His honour to the greatness of his name*
> *Shall be, and make new nations.*

In the next reign, with the Virginia colony settled if not entirely secure and then only, exploration, settlement and the wealth of London were found in successful alliance, and in success were able to strengthen their union.

But, long before the death of Elizabeth, England had lost her parochial mentality. The far corners of the earth were no longer so far away, the desire to travel and to explore had been planted in the English character, and the gossip and the idiom of voyaging had taken root in the English intellect, so that Shakespeare, never an esoteric writer, could describe Malvolio as smiling 'his face into more lines than are in the new map of the Indies', and expect and receive the easy comprehension of his audience.

For the solid tasks of the first years of the seventeenth century, the merchant-buccaneers, the fighter-dreamers and the corsair-patriots of the sixteenth century had made excellent preparation.

WORKING MEN'S COLLEGE
★ LIBRARY ★

XV

SPORTS AND PASTIMES

SYDNEY CARTER

In Tudor times England was still described as 'Merry'.
What exactly was it doing to deserve this title? Any
accounts of the sports and pastimes of previous ages
had been written in manuscript; copies were few, and
most of them have perished. But from the beginning of
the sixteeth century there began to pour from the new
printing press books about hunting, hawking, archery,
swimming, fencing, dancing, chess and games of every
variety. Besides such manuals as these there are still
extant ballads, broadsides, printed plays and books of
every sort which throw light on the pastimes of the period.
For example, the dour-minded Philip Stubbes disap-
proved of nearly all the ways in which his countrymen
enjoyed themselves, and described them all in lurid detail.

What, then, are English men and women doing when
the curtain rises on the sixteenth century? The Tudor
monarchs, like their predecessors, hunt, hawk, dance, ride,
are fond of pageantry and keep a jester. Their greater
subjects do the same. Their lesser subjects drink ale
and dance upon the village green as they have done from

time immemorial; as for five hundred years at least, cock-fighting and bear-baiting delight them; and they still break their necks and noses playing football when they should be practising archery. North of the Tweed, king and commoner alike are already trying to hit a small ball into a distant hole. The English are not yet interested; but in Scotland golf and football are already bracketed as the two main reasons for the neglect of archery. As early as 1457 a royal ordinance had decreed (without success) 'that the futball and golf be utterly cryit down'.

Many games we know to-day are named already: besides golf and football, and pastimes such as running, jumping, swimming, wrestling, riding, hunting, fishing and shooting (with bow and arrow; as yet only rarely with a gun), references are found to tennis, billiards, bowls, dicing and card-playing, even to a game called cricket. Few of these games, it is true, were played according to the rules as we know them. Tennis was played on a hard court and usually indoors; between the inner and the outer wall of the court was a sloping ledge, or 'penthouse', as well as holes or 'hazards' in the wall. 'Real Tennis' (for which it is still possible to get a half-blue at Oxford) and not lawn tennis is the lineal descendant of this game. Henry VIII was an enthusiastic player, and the court he used can still be seen at Hampton Court.

Football, too, is not the game it used to be. Here is what Stubbes says about the way it was played in 1583:

'As concerning football playing I protest unto you that it may rather be called a friendlie kind of fight rather than a play or recreation—a bloody and murthering practice than a fellowly pastime or sport. For dooth not everyone lie in waight for his adversarie, seeking to overthrow and picke him on the nose, though it be on hard stones, on ditch or dale, on valley or hill or whatsoever place soever it be he careth not, so he have him downe; and he that can serve the most of this fashion he is counted the only fellow, and who but he?'

There seems to have been no limit to the size of the pitch or to the number of players on a side. The idea seems to have been to get the ball to the goal—which might be a gate, a haystack or anything—by any method, fair or foul; the game might range, and often did, from one end of a village to another. Prudent men avoided football, for, as Stubbes goes on to tell us: 'Sometimes their necks are broken, sometimes their legs, sometimes their noses gush out blood, sometimes their eyes start out.' Stubbes was not alone in his condemnation of football: Sir Thomas Elyot, in his famous work *The Governour* (1525) considers it too dangerous to form part of the education of a gentleman; James I also, who approved of manly games on principle, excepted football, which he called 'a laming exercise not to be used by a prince'.

Hunting must have been less artificial and less restricted than it is to-day. Large tracts of the countryside were still not enclosed. There were far fewer people in England then, and far more wild animals. Foxes were so common that they were considered vermin, to be killed by anyone in any manner possible, and the distinction of being 'a beast of venery', to be hunted with due pomp and ceremony, was reserved for the stag, the hare, the boar and the wolf. The last two were already rare in England, but the first two were plentiful enough. The quarry was pursued either with hounds alone, with bow and arrow, or with both. Shakespeare, according to local legend, poached the deer in St. Thomas Lucy's park, and had to leave Stratford on account of this. As in earlier centuries, hunting was a favourite sport of the court and the nobility. Queen Elizabeth, like her father, was devoted to it: even at the end of her long reign she is described as 'well and excellently disposed to hunting, for every second day she is on horseback and continues the sport long'.

Closely allied to hunting was the sport of hawking. The art of taming birds of prey and using them in order to kill other birds is supposed to have come originally from the east, where it still flourishes. It had reached Europe in the classical period; in the Middle Ages, it was extremely popular; to-day, owing no doubt to the development of the shot gun, it survives only as a curiosity. The bird normally used for hawking was the peregrine falcon; though the taming of a golden eagle, which Captain Knight has achieved in this century, is a novelty which would no doubt have pleased James I, who was always trying to improve not only his subject's minds and morals, but their games as well. In Tudor times hawking was still at the height of its popularity. This is attested not only by the number of books which were printed on the subject, but also by the extraordinary number of allusions to this sport in Shakespeare. *The Taming of the Shrew*, for example, is packed with hawking metaphors, similes and puns.

Horse-racing did not enjoy the popularity which it was to achieve under the Stuarts and was one of the few activities which did not feature in the famous celebrations on the occasion of Queen Elizabeth's visit to Kenilworth; though we know that it existed, for it is mentioned as being out of fashion. Horsemanship was cultivated, for it had a highly practical application, especially in battle; in this, as in so much else, the Italians were the schoolmasters of the rest of Europe, and *The Fower chiefyst offices belonging to Horsemanshippe,* published in 1566, was a translation from the Italian. As long as the horse was useful rather than ornamental, strength and manageability were probably more important qualities than speed. Henry VIII introduced a number of laws to improve the breed of British horses, mainly, no doubt, for military purposes; but his only criterion seems to have been size.

Greyhound racing, on the other hand, was popular; and in the sixteenth century, as now, heavy stakes were sometimes laid. Coursing was one of the sports—jumping, wrestling, cudgel-playing, sword and buckler, pitching the bar, throwing the sledge-hammer were others—included in the famous Cotswold games which took place each Whitsun from the end of the sixteenth century. Other outdoor games which have survived in some form to the present day are Prisoners' Base, Barley-break (also known as Last-in-Hell), Hide-and-Seek, Leap-frog, Skittles, Quoits and Troll-madam (which consisted of rolling balls into holes or arches). The Wild Mare was none other than the see-saw; while whipping tops, then as now, came into season in March. But tops had another function too: an enormous 'town top' was kept in many parishes, and the unemployed were set to whipping it. Merels, of which Nine Men's Morris was a variant, started as an outdoor game, the 'board' consisting of three or more squares, one inside the other, marked upon the ground; each player had a number of pegs and the idea, as in the simpler game, of noughts and crosses, was to get three of them in a row.

Of sixteenth-century indoor games, many are still played in public-houses or at children's parties. Shovel-board is shove-halfpenny, though it was then played with a shilling. Dicing and cards were well established, and already a target for the moralists. The different ways of playing dice, such as Hazard, Mumchance, Tray trip and Novum quinque, and the different kinds of card game such as Primero, Maw, Gleek and Trump, are, in most cases, little more than names to us; methods of cheating, however, do not seem to have changed a great deal. Dice could be loaded with quicksilver, their sides could be shaped unevenly, or they could be thrown in such a way that one knocked up against another in a manner calculated to leave the desired number uppermost. *A Manifest Detection of Dice Play* tells us what can take place at cards: 'Some play uppon the prickes, some pinch the cards privily with their nayls,—some turne up the corners,—some mark them with fine spots of inke.' Hoodman Blind is the same as Blind Man's Buff. Hot Cockles, in which one player hid his eyes and then was forced to guess who had him, though played in the sixteenth century by milkmaids, must be the ancestor of many hearty nursery games of to-day.

Although the names and even the rules of so many sports and pastimes have survived there have been some striking changes since the sixteenth century. This is true not only of the games, but also of the attitudes and tastes of the people playing them. This becomes clear when we consider some of the pastimes which have not survived.

First, bear-baiting. To chain a bear to a stake and then set half a dozen savage dogs to worry him is not the modern Englishman's idea of sport. Still less would it be considered fair for half a dozen men to attack a blinded bear with whips. The modern Englishman (or woman) who takes pleasure in blood sports likes to think that the victim can fight back or run away; the spectacle of helpless suffering is not supposed to be enjoyable. Our ancestors were not so particular; some would say, not so hypocritical.

As they flocked to see a public execution so did they flock unashamedly to see an animal baited to death. Bear-baiting, it would seem, was a sport in which England was pre-eminent. English mastiffs were renowned for their courage and Erasmus, in 1506, was struck by the herds of bears which were kept in England for this sport. There is no doubt of its popularity. Henry VIII made the Mastership of the game of 'bears, bulls and mastiff dogs' a royal office. A century after its erection, Donald Lupton wrote of the chief of these, Paris Garden at Bankside (where there was both bear-ring and bull-ring), 'This may be better termed a foul den than a fair garden. It's pity that so good a piece of ground is no better employed. Here are cruel beasts in it, and as badly used; here are foul beasts come to it, and as bad or worse keep it; they are fitter for a wilderness than a city' (*London and the Country Carbonadoed*, 1632). Among these 'worse beasts', the bear-ring promoters, were the two theatre-managers who put on most of Shakepeare's plays: Philip Henslowe and Edward Alleyn. From 1604 they won a virtual monopoly by sharing jointly in the Royal Mastership. Queen Elizabeth was an enthusiastic patron of the sport. James I, as an experiment, tried baiting lions. When, toward the end of the sixteenth century the theatre threatened to take away customers, the Privy Council intervened, and, in 1591, ordered the closing of theatres on Thursday for the sake of 'the game of bear-baiting and like pastimes which were maintained by Her Majesty's pleasure and were suffering neglect'. A few voices were raised against the royal game, among them

N

the voice of that old spoil-sport Stubbes. 'What Christian heart', he asks, 'can take pleasure to see one poor beast rend and tear and kill another and all for his foolish pleasure? . . . I think the devil is the master of the game, bearward and all.' Puritan opposition in general, however, seemed less concerned at the cruelty of bear-baiting than at the noise it caused and the profane company which it collected, and the fact that it took place upon the Sabbath. Equally popular, and perhaps more widespread than bear-baiting, was cock-fighting. There were cock-pits in all parts of England; bets were laid on rival birds and a cock-pit, like a bear-garden, was a by-word for disorder.

If kindness to animals was not yet a distinguishing feature of the English character, neither was gloominess or self-restraint. The modern Englishman has earned the reputation abroad of 'taking his pleasures seriously', of bottling up his emotions, of not knowing how to enjoy himself. In the sixteenth century, his reputation was the opposite. 'The English', a French observer writes in 1558, 'are joyous and very fond of music.' 'They excel', writes a German, Paul Hentzer, 'in dancing and music, for they are active and lively . . . They are vastly fond of great noises that fill the air, such as the firing of cannon, drums, and the ringing of bells; so that in London it is common for a number of them that have got a glass in their heads to go up into some belfry and ring the bells for hours together.' Erasmus, a Dutchman, is surprised and delighted by the freedom of our English ways; by the old English custom, for example, of greeting guests, male or female, with a kiss.

Dancing and traditional buffoonery and dressing-up, especially on the frequent holy-days which broke up the working year, were the delight of all classes. Most of these festivals were hallowed by the Church; but a few, such as May Day, were transparently pagan in origin. Older, too, than Christianity were the Yule-tide Mummers, with their resurrection play, and—in spite of their name—the Morris or Morisco dancers, who played such a prominent part in summer festivities. The story that the 'Morisco' came from Spain in the fourteenth century, in the train of John of Gaunt's armies, may be true as far as the name of this dance is concerned, and some of its trimmings—the bells, perhaps—may have been imported at the same period.

Besides a great variety of country dances, some of which have survived and more of which, in recent years, have been revived, there were the dances of the court; most of them imported from France or Italy. Such were the Pavane, a grave and stately dance in which even a cardinal could take part without offence; the Branle (or Brawl), the Canary and the Galliard, all lively; the Dumps, a dismal dance; the Bergomask, an old Italian dance which Bottom proposes that two of his company shall perform; and the Lavolta, which seems to have been a kind of waltz or gallop in which the gentleman twirled his partner round and helped her leap into the air.

On dancing, Stubbes, as usual, has a few sour but illuminating comments. 'Did not', he darkly asks, 'the Damosell daunce before Kinge *Herode,* when the head of John the Baptist was cut off? She daunced indeed: And herein may they see the fruit of daucing, what goodnesse it bringeth.' Herod, however, only watched, says Stubbes; what if he had danced *with* her, after the modern fashion, 'hand in hand, cheek by cheek, with bussing and kissing, slabbering and smearing, most beastly to behold? insomuch as I have heard many impudently say that they have chosen their Wyves, and wyves their Husbands by dancing; Whych plainly proveth the wickednesse of it'.

The sixteenth century was one of transformation. The arts of war were being revolutionized by gunpowder, the arts of peace by the invention of the printing press. The discovery of America and the new route to the East put Britain in the middle of the map, instead of on the edge of it. Most important of all perhaps, this was the century in which Western Christendom was split in two. In 1500 England was Catholic; in 1600 it was Protestant. But so far as sports and pastimes were concerned, England was still mediæval and the shock of these world-shaking changes was not felt until the end of the century.

The first to feel it, when it came, were the more warlike pastimes. The noble sport of jousting was rendered artificial. No skill with the lance could have saved Sir Philip Sidney from the canon ball which laid him low at Zutphen. Tournaments still continued, and a King of France was even killed at one, but their frequency diminished as the century went on. Archery, however, was not affected quite so soon, for the long bow was still a more efficient weapon than the hand-gun. Ascham's *Toxophilus,* the standard text-book on archery, appeared in 1545. Bow staves were still imported in large quantities, and merchants were obliged to import four with every ton of merchandise and ten with every tun of wine; and in one year, 1571, two thousand were imported from Hamburg alone. Archery was still held to be a sport of national importance; practice was compulsory, and Henry VIII ordained that every male from 17 to 60 should be provided with a long bow and two arrows. Early training and continued practice were the essence of archery; it required a weight of 90 lb. to draw a six-foot bow. The combination of strength and skill required was not learnt easily, and it only needed the invention of a gun which was both effective and portable for archery to be abandoned for something easier. As it was, it was all authority could do to keep men at the butts on a Sunday afternoon.

On the art of fencing, the invention of gunpowder acted in an oddly stimulating way. As long as knights were covered up in armour, sword-play was at a discount; a blow from a lance, a mace or a battle-axe could do more damage. Swords, when carried, were either of the great two-handed variety (which could be wielded like a battle-axe), or, for those who fought on foot, the short sword with a cutting edge, used in conjunction with a buckler. With the invention of the cannon, armour became obsolescent; but with armour left off the sword became more dangerous. A lighter kind of weapon came into use, one devised for thrusting rather than for cutting, and fencing was studied as a science. In this, as in most things, it was the Italians who led the way. The first manual of fencing was published at Modena in 1531; the first in English, printed in 1595, was by an Italian. This new way of fighting, however, met with stiff opposition in England. As far back as the battle of Hastings, when the Thanes took their stand behind a solid wall of shields and hit all comers with a battle-axe, the Anglo-Saxons had a partiality for using the edge of a weapon rather than the point. (The use of the long bow was another matter.) Battles, they felt, should be won by brawn and courage, not by cunning. They looked askance at this new science whereby the better man might be defeated. Local exponents of the art of fighting had, in addition, an economic reason for resenting the influx of Italian teachers. George Silver, in 1599, wrote a book to warn his fellow-countrymen 'how they forsake their own naturall fight, that they may be casting off these weake, fantasticall and most divelish and imperfect fights and by exercising their own ancient weapons be restored, or atchieve unto their naturall and most manly and victorious fighte again'. He relates with glee how an Englishman, 'one *Austen Bagger* . . . not standing much upon his skill, but carrying the valiant heart of a gentleman' challenged an Italian fencing master to a fight armed only with a sword and buckler; and, although his adversary attacked him with a long two-handed sword, 'stroke up his heels, and cut him over the breech, and trode upon him'. In spite of this, the rapier gained ground in England.

To-day the educational qualities of sport are sometimes spoken of as if they were a specifically English discovery, and a recent one at that. The ancient Greeks, of course, were well aware of them; but in the Middle Ages there had been a divorce between the intellectual and the physical in education: the intellectual being considered proper for a cleric, the physical for a knight. By the time of the Renaissance, however, learning was no longer a monkish monopoly, nor was it considered beneath the dignity of a nobleman or prince to know how to read or write. This, in fact, was the age of learned monarchs; no English queen, before or since, could have cursed an ambassador in Latin like Queen Elizabeth. But if princes were now concerned to cultivate their minds, they did not cease to cultivate their bodies too; Queen Elizabeth, although a linguist, hunted, danced and shot with the bow and arrow also. Roger Ascham, Elizabeth's tutor, gained his position not for his Latin and his Greek, but because Henry VIII liked the book which he wrote on archery. In a list of 'noble exercises', the author of *The Scholemaster* includes:

> 'to ride cumlie: to run fair at the tilt or ring: to plaie at all weapons: to shote faire in bow, or surlie in gon: to vaut lustely: to runne: to leape: to wrestle: to swimme: to daunce cumlie; to sing, and play of instrumentes cunnyngly: to hawke: to hunt: to play at tennes, and all pastimes generally, which be joyned with labor, used in open space, and on the day light, conteyning some fitte exercise for warre, or some pleasant pastime for peace.'

Ascham, a lively pedagogue, lived up to his own precepts; not only was he fond of pastimes 'used in open space, and on the day light', but indoor games like dicing too; which (says Camden) is why he died in poverty.

The newly-discovered world of America contributed eventually one new pastime: the smoking of tobacco. More far-reaching were the repercussions of the Reformation; these, however, were not fully felt until the middle of the following century. Henry VIII's break with the Papacy was over administration rather than belief; he dissolved the monasteries and pocketed the revenues, but he continued to burn heretics. A number of saints' days were struck off the calendar, among them (not surprisingly, considering the reason for his death) that of St. Thomas Becket. But there were enough saints' days left to scandalize Stubbes and, what is more, they were still kept in the good old manner with Morris dancing, Lords of Misrule, and the sale of drink to pay for church expenses. Sunday, too, was still a day of pleasure, with cock-fighting, dancing and archery. The Maypole, chief target of the Puritans, still lorded the village green; and, though Stubbes might gnash his teeth, the lads and lasses still got up in the middle of the night to bring back garlands to adorn that 'stinkyng Ydol' on the first of May. The real, doctrinal reformation was on the way; by 1600 it had taken root in Scotland, and all the Popish, pagan, merriment of mediæval times was now arraigned before the grim tribunal of the kirk. South of the border it was to flourish for another fifty years.

WORKING MEN'S COLLEGE LIBRARY

XVI

DRESS

IRIS BROOKE

THROUGHOUT the Tudor dynasty fashion in dress both male and female changed rapidly. This was undoubtedly due to the stimulus of a widening knowledge of the world outside the British Isles, and to the discovery of America with her amazing stores of precious metals and gems. The accumulation of vast fortunes suddenly come by and equally suddenly squandered led the more adventuresome of all classes into a riot of unbridled extravagance, and such extravagance was displayed in the fantastic fashions and apparently casual use of all manner of precious stones as a personal ornament.

As the sixteenth century advanced, more and more money was invested in the glamorous silks and velvets, damasks, satins and cloth of gold and silver imported from other countries.

At the time of Henry VII's accession men of all classes were wearing long hose, or tights called stocks, low round-necked shirts, short jerkins or doublets and a longer gown or cloak for warmth.

The doublet was usually like a waistcoat, with or without sleeves and reaching to the waist, and the stocks were tied to this garment with a sort of bootlace called 'points'. Emphasis was on the legs, which could be parti-coloured or patterned in a variety of ways. The hair was often worn long or just to the shoulder, and small hats or caps decorated with a feather gave a jaunty air to the young gallant. Excess of fashion at this time was displayed by the tightness of the nether garments and the extreme brevity of the jerkin which in some cases finished with a frill at the waist. The more sober-minded covered their thighs.

Women's dress still retained something of the quality associated with the Middle Ages. Their waists were high and their gowns full and long, sweeping the ground behind, but their hair and head-dressing styles were undergoing a drastic change. The towering steeples and horns and plucked foreheads had given place to the gable head-dress now associated with the Queen on playing cards, and with this new frame for the face hair once more appeared. A freer style too was coming into vogue where women wore their hair in a net or coif.

By the time Henry VIII came to the throne, 1509, the cloth needed for a fashionable jerkin was some seven or eight yards where previously a mere two had been more than was necessary; the silhouette had entirely changed by the addition of a full gathered knee-length gown with wide shoulders, or a pleated skirt attached to the doublet with points, and full sleeves also added in the same manner. Bands of black velvet ornamented skirt and gown; these were called 'guards'. Large flat caps were more popular than the smaller one of a decade ago. These were slashed at the brim, following the prevailing fashion for

c 1490   c 1520   c 1540   c 1555

MEN'S CLOTHES OF THE EARLY TUDOR PERIOD

slashing everything. This slashing of garments to show a
contrasting undergarment or lining, was becoming a main
feature in men's fashions, to remain in some form or other
right through the Tudor period. Gradually throughout
Henry VIII's reign the shirt neck rose till some time in
the 40's a tiny ruffle appeared. As the shoulders grew
larger and the shirt neck higher long hair gradually
ceased to be worn, and by about 1520 the hair was rarely
seen below the ears. Shoes were square-toed and very wide
with little or no heel covering.

The variety of women's fashions that appeared during
Henry VIII's reign defy adequate description; every con-
ceivable form of sleeve had its place, puffed and slashed,
long and hanging in great folds across the forearm; open
and bell-like with embroidered undersleeves, or false
sleeves, fur sleeves and sleeves consisting of half a dozen
different bits and pieces—all ornamented or affixed with
jewels or points. About the only feature that predomi-
nated during this time in women's dress was that the
bodice or stomacher was tight-fitting round the ribs and
finished in a low square neck. Even the waist varied from
its natural position to one several inches higher, and the
neck-line of a shift or undergarment could be as low and
revealing or as high and prim as personal whim governed.
Skirts were all long and often had a train at the back
lifted and tied at the waist; they might be pleated tightly
in vast folds round the waist or made from such heavily
embroidered material that they could be only eased into
the waistband. By about 1525 the skirt was sometimes
split up the front to show a contrasting petticoat. Hair-
dressing was informal, a mesh net usually holding the hair
in place, though young girls were often seen with their
hair showing long underneath the coif and veil, or gable

WOMEN'S CLOTHES OF THE EARLY TUDOR PERIOD

head-dress. Hats and caps after the masculine fashion were very popular.

Between 1540 and 1550 the riot of individual expression in dress had settled into an accepted formula. A tight square-necked stomacher or bodice was usually worn over a leather corset. This had bell-shaped sleeves over a heavily embroidered undersleeve which tied to show puffs of the shift beneath. The skirt was split up the front displaying a fine petticoat. The coif had developed into an upstanding semicircular head-dress with veil behind.

The male silhouette was practically square from shoulder to mid-thigh; pleating, slashing, padding, fur and heavy materials all combining to give the strange effect inseparable to our vision of Henry VIII. This effect was, however, achieved more by the wearing of a sleeveless gown or mock-coat (the latter being a cloak with sleeves for ornament only) over the 'stocks' and jerkin. The neck of the jerkin or doublet had now risen to the throat, where collar or ruffle showed.

A word here must be said of the 'stocks'. These nether garments were in theory the same as the slashed hose of half a century earlier, and though to all appearances they were two garments—stockings and breeches—they were in reality all one, the top sections round the thighs being slashed and padded or ornamented with strips of material called panes, through which a lining appeared. This lining could be arranged to please the wearer, pulled out in puffs or barely showing; these were called trunk-hose.

Edward VI's and Mary's reign showed little alteration in the women's costume just described, but the marriage of Mary to Philip of Spain quickly showed itself in the almost instantaneous change of the Henry VIII silhouette

c 1565   c 1575   c 1590   c 1600

MEN'S CLOTHES OF THE LATE TUDOR PERIOD

to that of the Spanish gallant. By the time Elizabeth came to the throne, the Spanish styles for men had got a firm hold—high hats of fine beaver, ruffles, jaunty short cloaks—were more popular than flat caps and wide shoulders. Shoes had lost their duck-bill shape and now fitted the foot. The short jerkin, finishing some five or six inches below the waist, displayed the trunk hose to advantage, and the young man with fine limbs was once more tempted to display them, accentuating their elegance by padding the trunk part to excess. Wool, horsehair, bran and even rags were used to obtain the fashionable pumpkin-like contour. The German version resembling slashed plus-fours were called plunder-hose, for the soldiers found them a useful place for storing loot.

As might be expected the young Queen was quick to throw away the established fashions of her sister's short reign, and her growing interest in clothes became an unbridled passion as the century advanced. No new style was too ostentatious or ornate, and on her death we are told that her wardrobe held 3,000 gowns.

Starch was introduced to this country in 1564, and from that time to the end of the century ruffles gradually grew in size. Bonnets and caps were also starched and the heart-shaped cap associated with Mary Queen of Scots was a particularly charming and popular fashion. The hair was now being done up on the top and back of the head, brushed back from the face and no longer necessarily parted in the middle. Hats were worn over a tiny bonnet. The bell-shaped sleeve totally disappeared with Mary, and a full puffed sleeve from shoulder to cuff, or a puff high on the shoulder and a long tight sleeve took its place.

The Spanish vertingale or hoop at the bottom of the

petticoat gave a new bell-like shape to the skirt, which now barely touched the ground. Tight corseting had come into vogue. Mantles or surcoats were worn with short puffed sleeve and a shoulder yoke from which these garments gradually spread out to the full hoop of the skirt falling in heavy formal lines from shoulder to hem.

At some time between 1570 and 1575 the existing fashions began to be stormed by a variety of continental absurdities and exaggerations. Chief amongst those for men was the 'peascod-belly' doublet—a short doublet finishing just below the waist in a padded and stiffened protuberance over the stomach still seen to-day on the figure of Punch. This fashion became fantastically exaggerated during the 80's. Shoulders were accentuated with a sausage-like roll of material which was cut in places and called 'picadills'. Varieties in nether garments introduced during this decade included 'Venetians' and trunk-hose with canion. These introductions, however, did not oust the now familiar trunk-hose which remained in favour until the 90's. The former were a species of knee-breeches, padded, quilted and bombasted from waist to knee where they were tied with a wide garter or finished with a decorated band.

Trunk-hose with canions were made like the ordinary trunk-hose only cut off just below the knee and a separate stocking worn over them, which was tied with a garter either just below or above the knee—thus giving the appearance of three separate nether-garments, for the canion was often made of patterned material. Beaver hats and tall velvet caps were a fashionable extravagance and the hat-bands and jewels which went to their decoration were often of some considerable value.

The most outstanding change in women's clothes that

took place at this time was probably the introduction of the French vertingale or farthingale—a gigantic cartwheel-like affair attached at the waist and tipped forward slightly so that the skirt formed a drum-shape rather than the bell-shape of the Spanish farthingale, and was just long enough to show the new thick-soled shoes.

These vast skirts were often worn with a sort of frilled basque at the waist that finished at the hoop. To accommodate this ungainly contraption and keep the required tilt in front, the stomacher was boned and pointed and sometimes, in the more exaggerated styles, a false stomacher was worn apparently loose from the breast and resting on the tilted front of the farthingale. In several portraits of the time the hand is hidden behind this false V. The introduction of the French farthingale did not in any way affect the popularity of the now well-established Spanish version. As long as the skirts were held out in a suitably exaggerated style to balance the gigantic ruffles and bombasted sleeves and display the increasingly large patterns with which most materials were ornamented—fashion was being served adequately.

The now familiar employment of starch produced yet another fashionable garment. A transparent cobweb lawn veil or cloak with a large heart-shaped collar that stood up behind the ruffle and was usually ornamented with a tiny band of lace at the edge.

The ruffle itself after 1580 was often worn open in front and when worn with the French farthingale it frequently divided and was carried down to the bottom of the V stomacher.

Hair styles widened and became more ornate during the 80's. Curling and crimping alone soon ceased to give the exaggerated effect required, and wire frames were

c 1575   c 1585   WOMEN'S CLOTHES OF THE LATE TUDOR PERIOD   c 1600

devised to support the frizzed hair which was augmented by the addition of false locks. Wreaths of imitation flowers or jewels were arranged across the curled and padded hair and within a few years, of the fashion for hair rather than head-dress, wigs and hair dyes were in vogue. Pearls, beads, and precious stones were fixed in profusion amongst the curls. On top of all this was worn a jaunty velvet or beaver hat with a high bulging crown and tiny brim; also decorated with jewels and feathers.

Embroidered and perfumed gloves and embroidered shoes made their first appearance in the later half of Elizabeth's reign.

This survey has now brought us to the last ten or twelve years of the Tudor dynasty which are remarkable for their exotic and ostentatious display—such a display of personal finery has never before nor since occurred in the history of English costume.

Pattern ran riot and decoration and ornament seemed to know no bounds. It is in fact impossible to exaggerate the profusion of detail that decorated every item of apparel at this time. Practically every square inch of material was crowded with ornament in some form— jewels, embroideries, lace, guards, gold eyelet holes and tiny slashes through which puffs of lining could be pulled out. Each ensemble might consist of five or six different sorts of materials, e.g. sleeves of velvet, lacing over a silk undersleeve, a stomacher of gold embroideries, a gown of taffeta embroidered with weird monsters from other countries worn over a petticoat guarded with velvet and lace. A fine transparent lace collar and cuffs, embroidered gloves, stockings and satin shoes, complete the outfit.

Men's fashions during this decade were equally exotic

and fantastic and practically every type of nether-garment appeared during these few years, including what was then called 'open breeches'—the forerunner of those loose-flapping 'shorts' worn by the cavalier of Stuart times. Not to be outdone in fantasy by women's fashions, a new wired and stiffened type of trunk-hose with canions became the male version of the farthingale. This resembled a giant cheese from waist to mid-thigh.

When the 'peascod' doublets ceased to be fashionable another type of doublet with a slightly armorial effect became the vogue. This effect was achieved usually by a padded lining and the bottom of the doublet was finished with overlapping tabs from the waist, giving much the same appearance as the 'tassets' worn on armour. The shoulders were nearly always finished with a roll of cut or decorated material, rather like an epaulet. Short cloaks with high stiffened collars were nearly always worn; shoes were for the first time made with high heels. Hats of all shapes and colours from a twelve-inch high chimneypot of black beaver to a russet velvet cap trimmed with a hat-band of gold and pearls. The ruffle was beginning to disappear and an open-fronted collar of starched lawn or lace became the resting-place for the fashionable 'lovelock' which young gallants were beginning to grow. This 'lovelock' was usually an isolated lock of hair that grew from one side of the head only; the rest of the hair was kept short.

Throughout Elizabeth's reign fashion, which had during the Middle Ages been the prerogative of the wealthy only, had penetrated to all classes, and even the peasant and his wife were happy to sell their last pig so that they might appear on Sunday clad in the starched ruffles and farthingales that were so popular. England was enjoying a period of immense wealth.

It was only the unadventuresome who toiled unprofitably, for fortunes were to be made at home from wool as well as from foreign merchandise and pirating on the high seas.

The Englishman was still a craftsman and if his exuberance and new-found wealth outbalanced his taste in dress, it was but a sign of the times; each item of clothing, individually, was an artistic achievement, each pattern perfect in its execution; weaving, lace-making, and embroideries were at their best—it was indeed the conglomeration of too many ideas that rendered their apparel so incongruous.

WORKING MEN'S COLLEGE LIBRARY

SUGGESTED LIST OF BOOKS
FOR FURTHER READING

I. GENERAL

L. F. SALZMAN, *England in Tudor Times*. 1926. Perhaps the best general introduction to the period.

J. A. WILLIAMSON, *The Age of Drake*. 1946. An authoritative account of the later Tudor period by an author whose outlook is never insular.

M. REESE, *The Tudors and Stuarts*, 1940. An introductory text-book, but sound.

KEITH FEILING, *England Under the Tudors and Stuarts*. 1926. A brilliant short essay in the Home University Library.

E. M. W. TILLYARD, *The Elizabethan World Picture*. 1943. Admirable, but probably too short for the material it covers.

H. MAYNARD-SMITH, *Pre-Reformation England*. 1938. Useful and encyclopaedic, but by no means literary.

L. EINSTEIN, *Tudor Ideals*. 1921. An American scholar's work that is now difficult to obtain in England. It contains a considerable amount of unusual material.

G. M. TREVELYAN, *English Social History*. 1944.

J. A. FROUDE, *History of England*. 1856–70. Superb in its own prejudiced manner.

A. F. POLLARD, *Factors in Modern History*. 1907. Contains some valuable and stimulating chapters.

C. T. ONIONS (Ed.), *Shakespeare's England*. 1917. An essential companion to all Tudor studies. It includes long authoritative essays on many aspects of life in England at the time.

J. Dover Wilson, *Life in Shakespeare's England.* 1911. An ordered anthology of contemporary writing. Actor, sailor, courtier, cheat, traveller and beggar tell in their own words what it was like to live in England in the sixteenth century.

J. B. Black, *The Reign of Elizabeth.* 1936.

S. C. Bindoff, *Tudor England.* 1950.

II. POLITICAL AND CONSTITUTIONAL DEVELOPMENT

H. A. L. Fisher, *Political History of England (1485–1547).* 1906.

A. F. Pollard, *Political History of England (1547–1603).* 1913.

D. L. Keir, *Constitutional History of Modern Britain.* 1938.

W. Notestein, *The Winning of the Initiative by the House of Commons.* 1926. An admirable lecture, edited with useful notes.

K. W. M. Pickthorn, *Early Tudor Government.* 1934. By no means easy to read, but essential for anyone seriously interested in the subject. Volume 2 (*Henry VIII*) is particularly valuable.

C. H. Williams, *The Tudor Despotism.* 1935. Easy reading and very stimulating.

K. M. Gwatkin, *Church and State in England to the Death of Queen Anne.* 1917. Still a very useful book.

A. F. Pollard, *Evolution of Parliament.* 1926.

J. R. Tanner, *Tudor Constitutional Documents.* 1922.

J. W. Allen, *Political Thought in the Sixteenth Century.* 1928. Only in part on England.

A. J. Carlyle, *Political Liberty. A History of the Conception in the Middle Ages and Modern Times.* The English material in this fifteenth- and sixteenth-century volume is scattered but valuable.

A. P. D'Entreves, *Mediæval Contributions to Political Thought.* 1935. Two of the six lectures on the sixteenth century are principally English. D'Entreves is particularly brilliant on Hooker.

H. W. DONNER, *An Introduction to Utopia.* 1945. A useful and easy small book by a learned Swede (written in English).

L. V. BAUMER, *Early Tudor Theories of Kingship.* 1940. Very learned American scholarship carried lightly. There is little better for the period up to 1550 and the book covers a great deal besides kingship.

J. E. NEALE. *The Elizabethan House of Commons.* 1949.

III. RELIGION

G. BASKERVILLE, *The English Monks and the Suppression of the Monasteries.* 1937. Revolutionary, but fascinating and quite essential.

DAVID MATTHEW, *Catholicism in England.* 1936. A Roman Catholic Archbishop and historian gives his view of the Catholic tradition throughout English history.

A. O. MEYER, *England and the Catholic Church under Queen Elizabeth.* 1911 (trans. 1916). The best Catholic book on the subject written by a German scholar.

E. G. RUPP, *Studies in the Making of the English Protestant Tradition.* 1947. Most interesting little book and particularly useful as counterweight to such historians as Matthew and Meyer.

W. HALLER, *The Rise of Puritanism.* 1938. Probably the best of many American books on the subject and the few pre-1600 chapters are extremely good.

F. M. POWICKE, *The Reformation in England.* 1941.

J. V. P. THOMPSON, *Supreme Governor.* 1940.

IV. TOWN LIFE AND COMMERCE

G. N. CLARK, *The Wealth of England (1496–1760).* 1946. A short useful study in the Home University Library series.

M. ST. CLARE BYRNE, *Elizabethan Life and Town and Country.* 1925. An admirable semi-popular work.

G. UNWIN, *Studies in Economic History.* Ed. by R. Tawney. 1927.

G. Unwin, *Industrial Organization in England in the Sixteenth and Seventeenth Centuries.* 1904. The former book has much interesting material on the Merchant Adventurers and on the cloth trade, etc., and the latter, though perhaps not quite so exciting, is the standard work on its subject.

Sir W. J. Ashley, *The Economic Organization of England.* 1914.

Sir W. J. Ashley, *Economic History, Part I, Volume II.* 1888–92.

R. H. Tawney & Eileen Power, *Tudor Economic Documents.* 1924.

F. P. Wilson, *The Plague in Shakespeare's London.* 1927. Obviously not essential, but a most interesting sidelight.

J. U. Nef, *The Rise of the British Coal Industry.* 1932. An enormous work, but a mine of fascinating information on a great deal besides coal.

H. D. Traill (Ed.), *Social England, Volume III.* 1897. Still a most useful symposium.

W. Cunningham, *The Growth of English Industry and Commerce, Volume II.* 1904. This volume is the least outmoded of his three and is still indispensable.

Camden Society (Ed.), *The Italian Relation of England.* A Venetian report on English manners and customs.

A. V. Judges, *The Elizabethan Underworld.* 1930.

V. COUNTRY LIFE AND ECONOMICS

Lord Ernle, *English Farming, Past and Present,* 1919, which includes his *Pioneers and Progress of English Farming,* 1912.

Lord Ernle, *The Land of the People,* Chapters 1 and 2.

H. C. Darby (Ed.), *Historical Geography of England.* 1936. The two chapters by E. G. R. Taylor are quite essential.

R. H. Tawney, *The Agrarian Problem in the Sixteenth Century.* 1912. A fascinating work, though Tawney has probably changed many of his views since he wrote it.

R. H. Tawney, *Religion and the Rise of Capitalism.* 1926.

H. D. Traill (Ed.), *Social England.* 1897. See above, under Section IV.

MILDRED C. CAMPBELL, *The Elizabethan Yeoman.*

A. L. ROWSE, *Tudor Cornwall.* 1941.

WILLIAM HARRISON (Ed. F. J. Furnival), *Description of England.* 1908.

VI. EDUCATION

ROGER ASCHAM, *The Scholemaster, or plaine and perfite way of teaching children to understand, write and speak in Latin tong.* 'Specially prepared for the private bryng-ing up of youth in gentlemen and noblemen's houses', it was inspired in part by the 'strange news that divers scholars of Eaton be run away from the schole for fear of beating', and includes a plea for gentleness in educa-tion as well as an ardent defence, in excellent English, of the use of the English language. First published in 1570 and edited by W. A. Wright in 1904.

JOHN CONYBEARE, *Letters and Exercises of the Elizabethan Schoolmaster* (edited by F. C. Conybeare, 1905).

SIR THOMAS ELYOT, *The Boke named the Governour.* Dedicated to Henry VIII, it is a treatise on the education of those destined for high office. First published in 1531, a scholarly edition by H. H. S. Croft appeared in 1880.

RICHARD MULCASTER, *Elementarie.* Reprinted in the 'Tudor and Stuart Library' in facsimile by the Clarendon Press in 1925.

J. BRINSLEY, *Ludus Literarius; or, the Grammar Schools.* Ed. 1917.

J. W. ADAMSON, *Short History of Education.* 1912. The 'standard' work.

W. H. WOODWARD, *Studies in Education during the Age of the Renaissance.* 1906.

FOSTER WATSON, *The English Grammar School to 1660: their Curriculum and Practice.* 1908.

VII. SCIENCE

SIR W. C. DAMPIER, *A Shorter History of Science.* 1944.

K. J. FRANKLIN, *A Short History of Physiology.* 1933.

E. J. HOLMYARD, *Makers of Chemistry*. 1931.

C. SINGER, *A Short History of Science*. 1941.

C. SINGER, *A Short History of Medicine*. 1928.

A. C. CROMBIE, *Augustine to Galileo*. 1950.

VIII. POETRY

E. K. CHAMBERS (Ed.), *The Oxford Book of Sixteenth Century Verse*. 1932. The outstanding and most accessible among innumerable collections.

NORMAN AULT (Ed.), *Elizabethan Lyrics from the Original Texts*. 1925.

GERALD BULLETT (Ed.), *Silver Poets of the Sixteenth Century*. 1947. Almost the complete works of Wyatt, Surrey, Sidney, Raleigh and Davies in an Everyman edition.

V. DE SOLA PINTO, *English Renaissance, 1510–1688*. 1938. An admirable introduction with a comprehensive bibliography.

F. S. BOAS, *Songs and Lyrics from the English Song Books*. 1945.

There are various collections and selections from the works of all sixteenth-century poets. Critical comment on sixteenth-century poetry is an outstanding feature in English literary achievement. Among suggested books are:

GEORGE WYNDHAM, *Essays in Romantic Literature*. 1919.

F. P. WILSON, *Eliabethan and Jacobean*. 1945. Rather intellectualized criticism but extremely interesting.

D. BUSH, *The Renaissance and English Humanism*. 1939.

THEODORE SPENCER, *Shakespeare and the Nature of Man*. 1943. Probably the best book on Elizabethan philosophy.

IX. THEATRE

E. A. G. LAMBORNE & G. B. HARRISON, *Shakespeare, the Man and his Stage*. 1923. A wonderful short book, with a brilliant chapter on 'Shakespeare's Age'.

J. DOVER WILSON, *The Fortunes of Falstaff*. 1943. Probably the best book of a brilliant Shakespearian critic, with a great deal that is not merely on Shakespeare.

E. M. W. TILLYARD, *Shakspeare's History Plays*. 1944. It includes a great deal on the Tudor view of history.

G. GORDON, *Shakespearean Comedy and other Studies*. 1944. A most delightful book that contains a superb essay on the state of English at the time.

ALLARDYCE NICOLL, *The Development of the Theatre*. 1948.

AGNES MURE MACKENZIE, *Handbook to the English Renaissance Drama*. 1927.

BERNARD MILES, *The British Theatre*. 1948. A short essay on the whole history of British stage.

HARLEY GRANVILLE BARKER & G. B. HARRISON (Ed.), *A Companion to Shakespeare Studies*. 1934. Excellently written and informative essays on all aspects of Shakespearian scholarship. Invaluable for the reader who wishes to understand the relationship between the Elizabthan theatre and Elizabethan life.

J. DOVER WILSON, *Life in Shakespeare's England*. 1911. [See under General List.]

Many editions of individual playwrights include accounts of sixteenth-century theatrical technique and biographers of the writers. [See also under Poetry.]

X. PROSE

Specimens from most of the writers mentioned can be found in the collections indicated.

SIR THOMAS MALORY, *The Morte D'Arthur*.

ROGER ASCHAM, *Works* (ed. Wright).

TUDOR TRANSLATIONS (ed. Clements).

JOHN LYLY, *Euphues*.

SIR PHILIP SIDNEY, *Works* (ed. Feuillerat).

THOMAS DELONEY, *Works* (ed. Mann).

G. SAINTSBURY, *History of English Prose Rhythms*. 1912.

Cambridge History of English Literature, Vol. IV.

LATIMER, *Sermons*

TYNDALE, *New Testament* (Cambridge edition).

Shorter Elizabethan and Jacobean Novels (Everyman).

XI. PAINTING AND SCULPTURE

Seeing of course is more important than reading. This is simplest in London: the miniatures at the Victoria and Albert Museum; Holbein at the National Gallery, and a comprehensive cross-section of English painting at the National Portrait Gallery—but most provincial museums can show interesting examples. Any near-at-hand old country house that is open to the public should be visited.

Books:

C. H. COLLINS-BAKER & W. G. CONSTABLE, *English Painting of the Sixteenth and Seventeenth Centuries.* 1930. This is the basic work on the lesser painters: it does not deal with Holbein or with miniatures. Beautifully illustrated.

R. WORNUM, *Holbein.* 1867. An old work, but probably still the best general book in English.

K. T. PARKER, *Holbein's Drawings at Windsor Castle.* 1945.

A. REYNOLDS, *Hilliard Exhibition Catalogue.* Victoria and Albert Museum, 1947.

B. LONG, *British Miniaturists.* 1929.

CARL WINTER, *Elizabethan Miniatures.* 1946.

Sculpture is not concentrated in museums, but may be seen all over the country, particularly in old churches. MRS. ESDALE'S *English Monumental Sculpture since the Renaissance,* 1947, forms a good introduction, which may be followed up in other works by the same writer.

XII. ARCHITECTURE

J. A. GOTCH, *English Renaissance Architecture.* 1901. Still the standard book.

T. GARNER & A. STRATTON, *The Domestic Architecture of England during the Tudor Period.* Two vols. 1911; 1929.

XIII. MUSIC

As with Painting, seeing is more important than reading, so with Music listening is vital. There are a certain number of recordings of Tudor Music; the most accessible, and in many ways the best, are in the *Columbia History of Music*.

Books:

E. H. FELLOWES, *English Madrigal Composers*. 1921.

W. H. GRATTON FLOOD, *Early Tudor Composers*, 1925.

    Late Tudor Composers. 1929.

PETER WARLOCK, *The English Ayre*. 1926.

ERNEST MEYER, *English Chamber Music*. 1946.

PAUL H. LANG, *Music in Western Civilization*. 1942.

ERNEST WALKER, *History of Music in England*. 1907. Chapters III and IV contain one of the best accounts of music in Shakespeare's time.

XIV. VOYAGERS

J. A. FROUDE, *English Seamen in the Sixteenth Century*. 1895.

W. RALEIGH, *English Voyages in the Sixteenth Century*. 1906.

M. P. ANDREWS, *Virginia—the old Dominion*. 1937. Chapter I gives an excellent short account of early American exploration.

J. A. WILLIAMSON, *Maritime Enterprise (1485–1558)*. 1913. *The Ocean in English History*. 1941.

XV. SPORTS AND PASTIMES

P. STUBBES, *The Anatomie of Abuses*. Stubbes accidentally did a great service to history by recording the details of the customs that he attacked so vigorously.

R. ASCHAM, *Toxophilus*.

LADY GOMME, *The Traditional Games of England, Scotland and Ireland*. 1894-8.

D. P. BLAINE, *An Encyclopædia of Rural Sports*. 1840.

L. WHISTLER, *The English Festivals*. 1947.

XVI. DRESS

IRIS BROOKE, *English Costume in the Sixteenth Century*. 1933.

D. C. CALTHROP, *English Costume*. 1906.

WORKING MEN'S COLLEGE LIBRARY

BIOGRAPHIES

KATHERINE GARVIN (Ed.), *The Great Tudors*. 1935. Contains short biographical essays by various hands on most of the major (and many of the minor) Elizabethan figures.

A. L. ROWSE & G. B. HARRISON, *Queen Elizabeth and her Subjects*. 1935. A series of broadcast talks but, despite the limitations of the medium, extremely interesting.

CONYERS READ, *The Tudors*. 1936. Biographical essays on each king and queen.

E. FELLOWES, *William Byrd*. 1923.

EVELYN WAUGH, *Edmund Campion*. A Roman Catholic interpretation of the life of the Jesuit martyr, but excellent biography, brilliantly written.

J. H. LUPTON, *Colet*. 1887.

A. F. POLLARD, *Cranmer and the English Reformation*. 1904.

R. B. MERRIMAN, *Life and Times of Thomas Cromwell*. 1902.

G. B. HARRISON, *Robert Devereux, Earl of Essex*. 1937.

JULIAN CORBETT, *Sir Francis Drake*. 1890.

J. F. MOZLEY, *John Foxe and his Book*. 1940.

M. C. CREIGHTON, *Queen Elizabeth*. 1899. A Victorian view, but still the standard work.

J. E. NEALE, *Queen Elizabeth*. 1934. A stimulating modern biography.

LYTTON STRACHEY, *Elizabeth and Essex*. 1928.

PRESERVED SMITH, *Erasmus*. 1923. The standard work—and indispensable.

A. L. ROWSE, *Sir Richard Grenville*. 1937.

A. F. POLLARD, *Henry VIII*. 1902.

LORD EUSTACE PERCY, *John Knox*. 1937. A fascinating book, with much on England, and indeed Europe, as well as on Scotland.

J. BAKELESS, *Christopher Marlowe*. 1938.

H. F. M. PRESCOTT, *Spanish Tudor: A Life of Bloody Mary*. 1940.

R. W. CHAMBERS, *Sir Thomas More*. 1935. Among the very best of biographies. A keen study, well written.

BIOGRAPHIES

WILLIAM ROPER, *Life of More*. Contemporary account by More's son-in-law. Available in Everyman.

EDWARD THOMPSON, *Sir Walter Raleigh*. 1935. The best modern full-dress life.

ERIC ECCLESTONE, *Sir Walter Raleigh*. 1941. A remarkably good 'small' book.

D. B. QUINN, *Raleigh*. 1947.

E. K. CHAMBERS & CHARLES WILLIAMS, *A Short Life of William Shakespeare*. 1935. Very useful. All the available material in small compass.

PIERCE BUTLER, *Materials for the Life of Shakespeare*.

HAZELTON SPENCER, *The Art and Life of William Shakespeare*. 1940. Much the best modern American scholar's life.

W. L. RENWICK, *Spenser*. 1925.

J. F. MOZLEY, *William Tyndale*. 1937.

CONYERS READ, *Mr. Secretary Walsingham*. 1925. In three volumes.

A. F. POLLARD, *Wolsey*. 1924.

GEORGE CAVENDISH, *Life of Wolsey*. A contemporary life, by Wolsey's gentleman-usher. It is from this that the Wolsey of Shakespeare's *Henry VIII* is largely drawn.

WORKING MEN'S COLLEGE LIBRARY

1 6 NOV 1950

0 5 DEC 1950

1 3 JAN 1951

1 4 APR

23 MAY

2 5 MAY 1959
1 5 JUN 1959

WORKING MEN'S
COLLEGE
LIBRARY

AN 10999
CN 942·03
AC
TC PB
DC
D